FALWELL INC.

FALWELL INC.

INSIDE A RELIGIOUS, POLITICAL, EDUCATIONAL, AND BUSINESS EMPIRE

DIRK SMILLIE

ST. MARTIN'S PRESS ✵ NEW YORK

FALWELL INC. Copyright © 2008 by Dirk Smillie. All rights reserved. Printed in the United States of America. For information, address St. Martin's Press, 175 Fifth Avenue, New York, N.Y. 10010.

www.stmartins.com

Library of Congress Cataloging-in-Publication Data

Smillie, Dirk.
    Falwell Inc. : inside a religious, political, educational, and business empire / Dirk Smillie.—1st ed.
        p. cm.
    Includes bibliographical references.
    ISBN-13: 978-0-312-37629-1
    ISBN-10: 0-312-37629-4
    1. Falwell, Jerry.   2. Baptists—United States—Clergy—Biography.   I. Title.
BX6495.F3S65 2008
286.1092—dc22
    [B]

                                                            2008010610

First Edition: August 2008

10   9   8   7   6   5   4   3   2   1

For Martha

Contents

FALWELL INC.

INTRODUCTION

*The common denominator of all highly
successful people is a narrative of trouble.*

—JERRY FALWELL

O N the last morning of Jerry Falwell's life, he awoke at
6:20 A.M., slowly rolled out of bed, showered, shaved,
dressed, and sat down in his study to bang out a storm
of e-mail. It was Tuesday, May 15, just four days before the 2007
graduation ceremonies at Liberty University, the school he had
founded thirty-six years earlier. Former House Speaker Newt Gingrich would be coming to Liberty that Saturday to deliver the
commencement address to 3,598 graduating students. Among
them was the first graduating class of Liberty's law school. They
would assemble at Williams Stadium on the slopes of Candler's
Mountain in Lynchburg, Virginia.

Falwell wrote up a list of things to do that day and printed them
out. They included a call to the school's admissions office to arrange
a scholarship for a waitress he and Macel, his wife of forty-nine

years, met the night before at dinner. He folded and tucked the list into his suit pocket. Then he read a passage from Scottish theologian Oswald Chambers's *My Utmost for His Highest*. It said:

> "God is the master designer, and He allows adversities into your life to see if you can jump over them. . . . Rise to the occasion. Do what the trial demands of you. It does not matter how much it hurts as long as it gives God the opportunity to manifest the life of Jesus in your body."

Falwell paused and looked up for a moment, thinking about his own body. He had been battling sluggishness and shortness of breath every day for weeks. He was slowing down fast; recent medical tests had revealed that his advancing heart disease required intervention, and soon.

A little past 7 A.M. he called Ronald S. Godwin, Liberty's chief operating officer. "Ron, get your butt out of bed. I've got a dollar waitin' on a dime," cracked Falwell. Godwin was already awake and about to climb out from under the covers. They were to meet at the local Bob Evans, a country restaurant chain, at 8:30 A.M. that morning. The eatery, on a highway along the southwest border of campus, was where Falwell had met Godwin for breakfast nearly every day for the past nine years.

At 8 A.M. Falwell kissed Macel good-bye and trudged outside, sliding his six-feet-two-inch, 320-pound frame into a black Denali SUV. When he got to Bob Evans he parked a mere sixty feet from the door, yet had to pause to catch his breath before he went in. Still, he was jovial and talkative. He took his favorite corner seat next to the window, where waiter Paul Witt greeted him using his nickname, "Chuckles." Falwell considered jabbing Witt in the stomach with his fist, as he often did, but Witt knew to keep his distance. "Just the usual," said Falwell.

Falwell was soon joined by Godwin. Falwell's breakfast companion had been executive director of the Moral Majority, then an executive at the *Washington Times,* followed by a second tour with Falwell beginning in 1999. Godwin and Falwell would each bring a list of priority items to the table. Godwin would write his on lined legal paper; Falwell printed his out at home. "What we got done before breakfast every morning was probably more than what most of what corporate America does," says Godwin. "We were completely comfortable with each other and wonderfully productive."

Falwell's order arrived: a three-egg Cheddar cheese omelet, sausage links on the side, plus a jar of mustard (for the eggs). He tore into the omelet as Godwin began running down costs for expanding Liberty's online curricula to grades three through twelve; Falwell nodded silently at each dollar figure. It was a downward extension of the university's online education program. "I have a friend with a kid in private school who pays sixteen thousand dollars a year in tuition and has a two-hour commute," he told Falwell. "Our program would cost them five thousand dollars and bring their commute time to zero."

Falwell nodded. "It'll blow the doors off the home-school market," he said.

Next on Godwin's list: alert Falwell that some big names in distance learning would soon visit campus to explore taking an equity stake in Liberty's online curricula. "We could sell out and retain the brand name, or maintain majority ownership and bring on some of these investors," said Godwin. Either way, Liberty stood to reap several hundred million dollars.

Falwell wasn't so much concerned about which model to use as to how quickly it could happen. "Let's do it soon," he said. "I'm not buying any green bananas, Ron."

Liberty's online education program was Godwin's brainchild and the university's golden goose. The net profits from the online curricula were higher than those of the school's residential campus. Godwin had first come up with the idea at another breakfast meeting with Falwell, this one at Howard Johnson's. Falwell got so excited by the concept that he immediately called the president of the accrediting body for Southern schools, set up a meeting, and was on a plane later that day to seek temporary accreditation.

Hopping on planes at a moment's notice was something Falwell had done for thirty years. As they finished eating, Godwin had some travel in mind that had nothing to do with education. "Doc, how 'bout you and I take a flight this afternoon to the Cleveland clinic. Randy could drive Macel. By the time you get checked in, she'd be there." Godwin was suggesting they fly to the Cleveland hospital where, two years earlier, doctors had implanted a stent to clear a blockage in Falwell's coronary artery. Macel didn't like to fly, so Godwin would arrange for Liberty's chief of police, Randy Smith, to drive her to Cleveland.

Falwell glanced up at Godwin through his large aviator glasses, startled by his concern. Falwell shook his head. "Ron, there won't be any stents this time, they'll cut me wide open," he said. "We've got too much goin' on this week. Let me get through graduation first," he said. Godwin and Falwell finished breakfast at about 10 A.M., returning separately to their offices on campus. Falwell drove to the Carter Glass Mansion, a brick cottage on a hill overlooking the university. He picked up his messages, closed the door, and turned on his computer. He wasn't due at his next meeting for an hour.

Godwin had a Liberty seminary professor waiting for him. He expected to see Falwell again for an 11 A.M. meeting with staff from the Liberty Broadcasting Network and Falwell's son Jonathan, a pastor at Thomas Road Baptist Church. At 11:10 A.M. Godwin noticed his meeting was running long and that the usually punctual Falwell had not arrived to pick him up. As Godwin's faculty guest got up to leave his phone rang. It was a television staffer calling Godwin to remind him of the meeting he and Falwell were late for. After Godwin hung up, he called Falwell's direct line but got no answer. He got up to put his jacket on, planning to drive to Falwell's office, but before he reached the door he heard his phone again. This time it was Randy Smith, the police chief, who had gone looking for Falwell and discovered him unconscious in his office.

Godwin raced to his car and arrived at the Carter Glass Mansion just as Jonathan Falwell pulled up. Inside, a team of paramedics were huddled around Falwell, laying face up on the floor beside his desk. He was not breathing. The bridge of his nose was split open, but there was no sign of blood in the wound. It suggested that Falwell's heart had stopped suddenly, causing him to fall forward, striking his nose on the desk before sliding to the floor.

It was a rerun of an episode two years earlier, when Falwell suddenly lost consciousness during a car ride in Lynchburg. After going into respiratory failure, his heart had stopped beating for four minutes. Paramedics managed to revive him in a hospital parking lot. This time, attempts were made to bring Falwell back to life first in his office, then in the ambulance on the way to the hospital. Neither worked. At 12:40 P.M. doctors at Lynchburg General Hospital pronounced Jerry Falwell dead of cardiac arrhythmia. He was seventy-three.

Macel and her sons, Jerry Jr. and Jonathan, later joined by daughter Jeannie, a surgeon who had rushed to Lynchburg from her own hospital in Richmond, sat alongside Falwell's hospital bed for some time. Falwell had probably died minutes after arriving at his office following breakfast with Godwin. That afternoon Godwin sent word to the entire Liberty faculty, students, and Thomas Road Baptist Church members that an announcement would be made at 2 P.M. at the 6,000-seat church sanctuary, completed just a year earlier. The meeting was a madhouse; the room was packed, as Godwin made his sad announcement.

Two days later, on a cool and overcast afternoon, a pair of dark SUVs pulled up to the 500,000-square-foot Arthur S. DeMoss building near the center of campus. Its broad stairway leads to a Corinthian-columned entrance. There were perhaps two hundred people milling around, waiting for the family to arrive. Jerry Jr. emerged from the lead car with Macel by the hand. Jonathan stepped out of the second SUV with his wife and four kids. Altogether, fourteen Falwells, ringed by six Liberty security guards, scaled the steps for a private visitation.

Even on an overcast day the cavernous DeMoss lobby is drenched in light from the dome in its ceiling. Its cheery sky-blue walls and wedding-cake trim add an oddly whimsical touch to its staid interior. In the middle of the room, perched above its polished marble floor, lay Jerry Falwell in an open casket. Falwell's hands looked small and shriveled, accented only by a gold Liberty ring on his right ring finger. He lay in his trademark charcoal suit, white shirt, and crimson silk tie, his left arm gently embracing a King James Bible. His eyes, tightly shut, gave his face an expression of intense meditation. His fragile white hair was combed close to his head. The interior of the solid bronze casket was lined with white velvet; it sat upon the same bier Ronald Reagan's coffin rested on during his own funeral. It had been rushed from Washington overnight at the request of Jerry Jr. to honor his father's devotion to Reagan.

Just down the road, Falwell's office inside the Carter Glass Mansion sat undisturbed, the shutters closed, as usual. The walnut top of his colonial-style desk was marred by water stains from a second-story flood the office suffered months earlier. On the right side of his desk was a stack of books: Newt Gingrich's *Rediscovering God In America,* which Falwell plugged in his online column that month; *A Match Made In Heaven,* by Zev Chafets, a chronicle of common ground held by Christian evangelicals and American Jews; and Peter Lillbank's *George Washington's Sacred Fire,* a screed exploring the depths of Washington's Christian devotion.

Falwell's center desk drawer was crammed with half opened rolls of Certs and twenty-five-cent stink bombs. Even at seventy-three, he had delighted in silently setting them off as an unsuspecting victim sat nearby. On the floor under his desk was a Louisville Slugger baseball bat signed by former Liberty student Dave Benham. The opposing walls of his office were lined with artifacts from his life: Winston Churchill figurines; two six-packs of Donald Duck soda produced in the 1950s by the prior occupants of

Falwell's original church building; a 40mm round fired during Ronald Reagan's funeral procession. On a nearby wall was a blown-up photo of Falwell and Macel deplaning from Air Force Two. The occasion was George H. W. Bush's commencement address at Liberty in 1990.

Scattered about a next-door conference room were color aerial photos of Candler's Mountain and a schematic for the just completed monogram on its northwest slope. Just a few days earlier the letters "LU" had been spelled out by 4,000 tons of rock and brick covering 3.8 acres. It was one of Falwell's last projects. Against a wall was a framed copy of a *Forbes* story, "Prophets of Boom," the basis for this book. Falwell had recently reminded me that he, along with several Liberty board members, thought the story was crafted with a contemptuous tone and a condescending perspective. But there it was, ready to be hung.

I first met Jerry Falwell the previous summer, when we sat down in this same conference room with son Jerry Jr. and Ron Godwin to discuss the story. Falwell appeared suspicious. He leaned forward in his chair, cocked his head toward me, and interlocked the fingers of his catcher's mitt-sized hands. "Now tell me why a national magazine like *Forbes* would be interested in a small-town university like ours?" It was not a difficult question.

For twenty-five years, Falwell's name had been synonymous with the Religious Right, buoying the prospects of Republican presidential candidates and raising hundreds of millions for conservative causes. My *Forbes* editor, Tom Post, and I believed that Falwell's real legacy was only now unfolding. Liberty University, the evangelical Christian college he had founded in 1971, was on an $82 million building tear, transforming Lynchburg's small-town economy. Once in debt for $100 million and nearly forced into bankruptcy, Liberty was finally solvent, and was a money magnet. The school's online program alone was worth perhaps $400 million. Its law school was constructing an exact replica of the U.S. Supreme Court. Its debate team had outranked Harvard, Yale, and Princeton. Falwell's legal eagles had successfully knocked down Jefferson-based laws, which capped the growth of Virginia churches. Now Falwell and his two sons, Jerry Jr. and Jonathan, planned to turn a Liberty-owned mountain into a billion-dollar endowment. What Post and I wanted to know was: How was a man in the twilight of his celebrity—whose power peaked two decades earlier—managing to pull all this off?

Had you met Jerry Falwell in the early 1970s, you'd remember a man with piercing blue eyes, chestnut sideburns, and a small pompadour. By the 1980s, he had put on thirty pounds, his hair had turned silver and the sideburns were erased. The defining feature of his face was a pair of oversized glasses perched on a mountainous nose. In the 1990s, his jowl line dropped into an expanding double chin, which seemed to inflate around his entire neck, causing upward pressure on his earlobes, which flared slightly as he spoke. His face, said one writer, resembled a Thomas Nast cartoon of a Gilded Age plutocrat.[1]

Falwell's life was defined by an unrelenting *joie de war*. He was like a soldier who, frustrated with slow-moving battle lines, heaves homemade incendiary devices at the enemy, which explode in a frightening display. It energizes the troops but the front doesn't advance much. It's been twenty years since the Moral Majority disbanded but rates of abortion and divorce have changed little. Gay rights have advanced and pornography is now even more pervasive.

To his enemies Jerry Falwell was a homophobe and a misogynist. He was the pastor who blamed 9/11 on liberals, lesbians, and abortionists. A former segregationist, he had called Bishop Desmond Tutu a "phony." The same accusation was made against Falwell himself. One writer termed Falwell a pious bumpkin from the South; the "prince of skunk hollow." This latter pejorative made reference to a man who never really shed the bad-boy values of his rowdy upbringing in Lynchburg. He simply cloaked them in clerical garb, said his critics. During his career, Falwell was jeered as a fascist at Harvard, chased from a stage by rioting Pentecostalists, survived two fatwas, received dozens of envelopes stuffed with used condoms, traveled with bodyguards, and lived behind an eight-foot-high security wall. His mailbox was blown up four times.

Jerry Falwell was the most visible American evangelical of the twentieth century, and perhaps the most hated. It didn't matter, he reasoned, because back home his family, friends, fellow pastors, and church members knew the real Jerry Falwell. They remember the thousands of hospital visits over the years, the counseling he provided to young couples whose marriage had hit the rocks, his presiding over weddings and funerals, and his founding of homes for alcoholics and unwed mothers. They remember the bear hugs he gave to new students at Liberty, how he cried and prayed with chef Paul Prudhomme in his New Orleans kitchen over the death of his wife, and how he turned around a plane he was on in order to talk a man out of suicide.

The Jerry Falwell in this book doesn't fit neatly into either of these extremes. I've attempted to reveal another side of Falwell:

a religious entrepreneur who zealously built a spiritual empire in spite of the fact he was not good with money, who committed funds before he raised them, and who built an entire university on an unsustainable economic model. How did he do it?

Financial bailouts from wealthy donors helped, but only after Falwell had survived for years in the red. He managed not only to save his school, but also his own ministry by the sheer force of his own personality and his quest to destroy what he felt were ugly stereotypes about himself and his faith.

In doing so he escaped one of the great traditions of American evangelism: self-destruction. The twentieth century is littered with fallen men and women of the cloth, like Aimee Semple McPherson, the 1920s female evangelist whose ministry imploded when she tried to fake her own drowning at sea. Later came the sex scandals of Jim Bakker, Jimmy Swaggart, and Ted Haggard.

If Falwell ever had an affair, it was the best-kept secret in Lynchburg. He once said, "You may think I'm an extremist, but you have to be careful about where you are and who you are with. When I'm driving past a bus stop and see a lady waiting for a bus, unless I have my wife or some other adult in the automobile, I don't pick her up, even if it is raining." Falwell refused to close the door to his office when in the company of single women, not even when he was with Jeanette Hogan, his longtime personal secretary.

In this book, I've brought back to life moments of obsession, desperation, and inspiration that propelled Falwell's religious and educational ventures, the twin engines of his empire. Just a few months after I began my research—and after Falwell and his sons had agreed to cooperate—came Falwell's death. This book would now have a subplot: a succession story that forecasts how two brothers, Chancellor Jerry Falwell Jr. and Pastor Jonathan Falwell, now plan to expand their famous father's religious enterprises far beyond what he ever achieved.

1. A Small-Town Killing

In 1929, Garland W. Falwell relished his reputation as a hell-on-wheels outlaw from the sticks. His thundering black roadster churned up clouds of dirt as he sped 60 mph along Campbell Avenue, a sand-clay road that was the main southern thoroughfare into Lynchburg, Virginia. When sheriff's deputies gave chase they kept a safe distance behind him, dodging canisters of mustard gas Garland heaved out the window in a sorry attempt to cause a smokescreen. Garland parted his short, chestnut hair down the middle, wore bow ties, and kept the sleeves of his white cotton shirts rolled up. He resembled a pudgy Good Humor man.

Garland and his two brothers, Carey and Warren, all ran gas stations within a mile of one another just east of town. They didn't much like the local cops and the authorities didn't much like them. The Falwell boys thought nothing of settling a minor dispute with a two-by-four, or any other object lying around. One day a reporter at the local paper, the *Lynchburg News,* skewered Garland in a story that recounted his mustard-gas antics. When the writer had the temerity to stop at Warren's service station for gas one sunny afternoon, Warren recognized the scribe, grabbed a crutch from a crippled customer, and began walloping the journalist over the head. The reporter drove away—without his gas—but the account made page one the next day.

Warren's filling station was at the intersection of routes 10 and 18 (now U.S. Highway 460 and Business Route 501). His business card noted his shop offered "wrecker service and a good place to eat." He operated a passenger-bus line with Carey, using on-board, battery-powered projectors to play Charlie Chaplin movies for their riders. Carey managed the north-south routes; Warren the east-west lines. Garland, Jerry Falwell's uncle, managed his own filling station and helped Carey run an oil-distribution outfit he had started, along with a string of cafes. The Falwell boys earned a good living from these small-town enterprises but had a side venture that made them more money than their bus lines, restaurants, and gas stations combined. At the height of Prohibition they sold moonshine. The Falwells were the biggest distributors of illegal liquor in central Virginia.

Their gas stations were drop-off points for jugs of corn whiskey and peach brandy. You could buy gas for thirty cents a gallon or whiskey for eight dollars a gallon. Sealed in jam jars, brandy went for two dollars per pint. The booze came from camouflaged stills in the densely wooded outskirts of town and arrived in the bumpers of the Falwells' fuel trucks. One of Carey's top runners was Chauncey Spencer, then a bellhop at the Hotel Carroll. Chauncey's mother was Lynchburg's famed poet Anne Spencer, who hosted visitors like Paul Robeson and Martin Luther King Jr. at her Pierce Street home. Mrs. Spencer would have skinned her son alive had she known his hotel job was actually cover for filling booze orders for the Falwells. Chauncey delivered liquor to Lynchburg's top madams, who operated out of a stretch of homes along Fourth Street, and to "nip joints," the term used back then for small-time speakeasies. Carey's free-flowing booze probably minted one thousand entrepreneurs in Lynchburg. "Anybody with a box of Dixie cups and a bottle of liquor became a businessman," says Charles Bennett, Lynchburg's chief of police.

The only problem with distributing booze was, with plenty of the stuff around, it was tempting to partake. The older Falwell brothers could hold their liquor. Not Garland: drinking turned him belligerent and morose.

He was in such a state one October evening in 1929, when a verbal showdown with a group of college students turned into a near-deadly car chase. Garland fired forty rounds into the sedan of the fleeing students, one of whom would have fourteen shot pellets removed from his head. Falwell was charged with attempted murder.*

---

*That evening Garland was sharing a round of bourbon with his cousin Courtney Falwell and a friend in an alcove off the café. Six rambunctious students from two nearby colleges suddenly arrived, laughing and whooping it up. They were rich kids from out of town, well dressed and well spoken. Just the type of customer Garland despised. A skinny lad in a neatly pressed navy blue suit, 5-foot-10 Gustav Wiltshire walked over to a phonograph in the corner with two of the girls and put on a tune. They ordered soft drinks, then Wiltshire asked Garland whether some illegal "hooch" might be procured.

Garland, annoyed at the flippancy of these noisy strangers, replied, "Ah guess that

In the late '20s, violent crime like this rarely occurred outside the city. When it did, perpetrators were dealt with seriously. But Carey Falwell controlled some of the very hubs of Lynchburg's small-town economy. His restaurants and gas stations were everywhere and his liquor was consumed by the town's most powerful figures. A judge agreed to release Garland to family custody as he awaited trial. When his court date arrived two months later, so did the crowds. The trial drew forty witnesses and three hundred spectators. A jury convicted Garland of the comparatively minor offense of "unlawful shooting," sentencing him to prison for two years. Carey had hired a smart defense attorney for Garland, who appealed and got the sentence reduced to three months in jail and a one-hundred-dollar fine. Even that was too much for Garland to stomach. He escaped from custody eleven days later, setting off a statewide manhunt. His brother Warren returned him to authorities with a polite apology, promising he'd serve the rest of his time. The incarceration would mean little to him.

On the evening of December 28, 1931, a call came into the Campbell County sheriff's office complaining that gunshots had been fired near Garland's filling station. Only two deputies served the entire county back then; deputies drove their own cars and used

depends. Are ya'll revenoors?" The term was shorthand for "revenue agents" sent to crack down on illegal liquor peddlers. Newspaper accounts differ over the sequence of events but agree the conversation took a nasty turn. Five of the six students quietly filed out. Wiltshire lingered, returning one of the soft drinks to Garland, slamming the bottle down, complaining there was no booze in the soda Garland had served him. Then came the sound of chairs being knocked over, grunts and a scream from Wiltshire. One of the boys ran back to find Wiltshire flat on his back, blood splattered on the floor behind him. Wiltshire was pinned by Garland and his cousin as Garland ham-

their own guns. Radios weren't yet used in many rural areas so calls would be responded to only when an officer learned of it by periodic checks from a call box. At least an hour went by before Deputy W. A. Farmer and his partner climbed into Farmer's sedan to investigate. They had good reason to be concerned: the caller said the source of the trouble was, as usual, Garland Falwell. When police arrived that night they were astonished to discover Garland and two friends not shooting at anyone, but harmlessly setting off firecrackers. The police had no quarrel with Garland. But Garland suddenly had a beef with them. "Who called y'all? Was it Carey?" he screamed as the two deputies walked away. The officers denied it was Carey who made the call, but wouldn't reveal their tipster to Garland.

As usual, Garland was soused with whiskey. But that night he was also flying high on a drug called veronal, prescribed to him by a family doctor to ease pain from his ankle, which was mangled in a motorcycle accident a few days earlier. In his paranoid, semidelusional state he concluded that Carey had indeed ratted him out. The authorities had been summoned in response to Garland's antics a half dozen times in recent months. One complaint came from Garland's own wife, alleging he had beat her.

---

mered the side of Wiltshire's head with the end of the bottle. When the bottle popped out of Garland's hand, Wiltshire broke free and ran for the door.

The three girls had gone to get their car, but in the confusion one boy disappeared into a nearby field. Student Anna Hershey was behind the wheel and pulled up in front of the filling station just as Wiltshire emerged. Wiltshire jerked the rear door open and tumbled into the backseat. Garland burst through the filling station entrance in time to see the car peeling away. Spitting curses under his breath, he ran back into the restaurant, grabbed several pistols, and ordered his cousin to drive Garland's

Garland suspected his own family was turning against him. He reasoned that his older brother, once his loyal advocate, had tired of defending him and was scheming to lock him up. He would teach Carey a lesson for this blood betrayal.

Garland retrieved his favorite artillery, a pair of .32 pistols, from his car. He marched across the street to Warren's restaurant, where Carey sometimes lingered into the late hours. Like a drunken Jesse James, Garland burst into the restaurant with both pistols drawn, his muddy perception suddenly jolted by the familiar rush of adrenaline from the cold, deadly steel in his hands. He scanned the tables for Carey, but his older brother was nowhere in sight. Garland limped upstairs to an office, where he heard Carey on the phone. Carey was running down a list of arrival times with a dispatcher at the Lynchburg bus station, checking on whether his rigs had rolled in on time. "With the receiver still in my hand, Garland rushed in with two pistols, the muzzles of which looked as big as barrels, and accused me of calling Farmer," recalled Carey.

Watching the scene unfold was one of Carey's cousins, who yelled "Garland!" The one-moment-diversion was all Carey needed to spring from his wooden chair and bolt through a doorway leading to a back window. He opened it and lunged through the open-

roadster to the front of the station. The trio climbed into the car and took off in pursuit.

The two cars raced through the hills, careening around cow pastures and tobacco farms. Garland and his posse could see the taillights of the students' Model A sedan ahead; they gained on them quickly. With his cousin behind the wheel, Garland leaned out the passenger door with his loaded .32 and squeezed off a few rounds. The students tried to keep their heads down as they heard the crack of gunshots behind them, bullets pelting the car. Then came a *BOOM* and a blast of glass from the

ing, with Garland in hot pursuit. Garland rushed to the window, but Carey had vanished. The younger Falwell fired three rounds at the nearest tree as he cursed his brother and tried to scare him into the open. Garland squinted his eyes through the clouds of gunpowder in the night air, but there was no sign of Carey, who was crouched motionless behind another tree some thirty yards away.

Garland left the window, his whereabouts unknown to Carey, who turned and walked cautiously along Route 10. But like Cary Grant in *North by Northwest,* he was soon running again. Garland was back in his car and fast approaching from behind. Carey could hear Garland's roadster roaring in the distance. In the dim moonlight, Carey ducked behind a shed, and hid until his brother's headlights blazed by.

The road dark again, Carey started walking, shivering in the night air as he approached the home of one of his oil-company employees, Robert Johnson. He had recently loaned a shotgun to Johnson for duck hunting. In the pitch dark, he anxiously rapped the front door with his knuckle. "It's Carey, open up!" Johnson came to the door and let his boss in. "Garland's gone wild. I need ma gun, Bob," said Carey, who went to wash blood from his hand. One of Garland's shots had nicked a finger. Carey lingered a while,

backseat; Garland had switched to a shotgun. "Git to town, he's gonna kill us!" screamed one of the girls. The back of Wiltshire's head was suddenly gushing blood; one girl tugged his coat off of him and pressed the end of a sleeve into the wound. Hope was in sight; the road suddenly became paved. They were on the outskirts of Lynchburg.

The two cars rounded a curve, the stink of burning rubber in the air as Garland tried to steady his pistol hand, firing madly. He reloaded, then emptied his revolver again. Luckily for Wiltshire and his friends, Garland was a terrible shot and drunk besides. As

then picked up the long-barreled shotgun Johnson had set down on a table, along with two cartridges. Carey cracked open the barrel and popped in one cartridge. He left without a word.

Walking stealthily through the woods, Carey found his way back to Warren's filling station. He could see the lights on inside behind the silhouettes of his father, Charlie Falwell, and a cousin on the porch, who were keeping watch for Garland. Carey walked up to the building, shotgun at his side. "Where in hell is Garland?" asked Carey. Carey's father just shook his head. "The boy's gone mad," said Carey. "He's crazy on dope." The trio walked back inside Warren's restaurant and sat down at a table, as Carey asked his companions who had called the sheriff on Garland. Carey kept his hand on the shotgun.

A few minutes later, they heard footsteps outside. Carey felt the hair stand up on his neck; he knew his brother's limp. "Garland?" yelled Carey. "Leave them guns outside." Garland burst through the door, pistols again drawn, his glassy eyes casting about like a deranged animal. Carey's cousin and father, both unarmed, flew out of their chairs. Carey sprinted upstairs to Warren's office as Garland fired two shots in his direction. Carey turned toward the open doorway, cocked the hammer on his shotgun, and swallowed hard. There was no time to find cover or jump out the window

they rolled into Lynchburg, the shooting stopped. Garland had pumped some forty rounds into the students' car. Finally, he was out of bullets.

Officer J. C. Horsley was on patrol that evening, shivering off the icy night air as he walked down Court Street. He stopped, blinking in disbelief as the lead car, riddled with bullet holes and a rear flat tire, pulled up to the intersection of 12th and Court Streets. Hershey jumped from the car. "Help!... Help please!" she screamed, running toward Horsley as her heavy wool coat bounced on her skinny frame. Horsley calmed her down, then listened to her account of the chase, keeping an eye on the three occu-

again. "Boy, don't come up here!" yelled Carey as he heard Garland clambering up the stairs. Garland stepped through the door frame; the brothers weren't fifteen feet from one another. Carey stepped backward, tripping over Warren's desk as he pulled the trigger. At that range the shot hit Garland like a cannonball; the pellets from Carey's gun would have no time to disburse. The blast jerked Garland's body grotesquely backward into the door frame, one pistol tumbling from his hand down the stairs as his stocky body crashed to the floor. There was just smoke and silence—and a hole the size of a baseball just above Garland's heart.

For a moment Carey could hear Garland gasping, then nothing. Carey cautiously stood up and glimpsed at the carnage. Garland's blood had splattered across the entire middle of the open office door. Carey was dumbfounded; he felt short of breath. He knelt next to Garland, calling his name, but his little brother did not move. Charlie appeared at the top of the stairs. Carey looked up at his father, who said nothing, his hand covering his mouth as he stared down at the still body of his son. Carey gathered his wits and picked up the phone to call the county sheriff. It would be another hour before Farmer and his partner returned to Warren's filling station.

Carey was arrested and released on $10,000 bail. The next day a judge went over the events of that evening with Carey, the two

---

pants of the car behind Hershey's. Garland and friends climbed out of the roadster and walked up to Horsley, their hands deep in their pockets.

Shifting unsteadily on his feet, Garland explained his side of the story, claiming that the well-dressed students (who turned out to be the sons and daughters of some prominent West Virginia families) tried to rob the filling station of $200. It was not a convincing tale. Horsley arrested Falwell and his entourage, walking them to police headquarters, then to the basement of City Hall a few blocks away. The arresting officer discovered Garland's one-man armory: Horsley took two .32 caliber pistols

deputies, Carey's father, his cousin, and a handful of witnesses. Carey was found not guilty in Garland's death. He had acted in self-defense. But this single tragedy, occurring in a hair-trigger moment, eventually ruined Carey Falwell's life and left an indelible mark on the life of his son, Jerry.

NINE generations of Falwells have lived, worked, thrived, and died in Virginia over the past three hundred years. Their remains lay scattered in cemeteries in Goochland, Buckingham, and Campbell counties. Not much of their history is known before 1869, the year several generations' worth of records were destroyed in a fire at the Buckingham County courthouse. The Falwells' modern history begins in 1850, when Jerry Falwell's great-grandfather Hezekiah came to Lynchburg and bought most of the northern face of Candler's Mountain, an undulating series of peaks along the western edge of town. It is land where dozens of family businesses would sprout: tobacco farms, wheelwrights, blacksmiths, dairies, restaurants, filling stations, hotels, a trucking service, and even an airport.

The first Falwells likely arrived among early waves of English

---

from Garland's belt, plus a double-barreled shotgun, a six-shooter, and yet another .32 from Garland's car.

Garland was held by the Lynchburg cops until sheriff's deputies from Campbell County arrived. Since the alleged crime—attempted murder—had occurred in the county, the sheriff's department took Falwell into custody. Wiltshire was taken to the hospital, where he would remain for three weeks. Besides the shot pellets in his head, doctors found a five-inch knife wound in his back and the gash near his temple.

settlers landing at the Jamestown colony in the late seventeenth century. They apparently spelled their name "Falwelly," but dropped the "y" sometime before the mid-nineteenth century. It's unknown whether they sought religious freedom or came to strike it rich in the New World.

Jamestown was supposed to help England cut its reliance on expensive goods from other European countries by becoming a new source of cheap imports. Launched by a group of London investors called the Virginia Company, their three ships brought 107 colonists to the settlement in May 1607. Many of the carpenters, barbers, farmers, and bricklayers who came ashore that month didn't care much about highfalutin' aims to strengthen the English economy—their interest was in finding gold, a dream that quickly fizzled.

The émigrés decamped on an island inside the Chesapeake Bay, whose briny depths teemed with oysters, mussels, crabs, and rockfish. It was an oceanic Eden, except that it was also the hunting and canoeing grounds of 14,000 Algonquian Indians making up the tribes of the Powhatan Confederacy. The settlers fought one bloody skirmish after another with the Powhatans as they tried their hand at glassmaking and cultivating sassafras. They sent their meager shipments to the British Isles. Much of England was deforested, so the colonists tried cutting lumber and shipping it east. None of these ventures amounted to much. Then, in 1612, a tobacco entrepreneur named John Rolfe arrived and planted at Jamestown a South American variety of tobacco called Orinoco, which oozed a sweet tangy flavor when smoked or chewed. He cured it over a fire, then shipped two hundred pounds of the leaf back to England. Rolfe's business partners were astounded. It tasted just like the

Spanish varieties that were all the rage in London. Rolfe's partners sent word back to rev up production of the new crop as fast as possible.

Tobacco was planted everywhere: along dirt roads and hillsides, in home gardens, and even the new colony's cemetery. The Powhatans, whose culture revolved around the cultivation of corn, squash, and beans, were amazed at what little acreage settlers devoted to food crops for their own survival. The new cash crop astounded the colonists, too. Their tobacco harvests would be the seeds of the very economic foundation of Virginia, creating unimaginable wealth for the South over the next 250 years.

The early Falwells are believed to have owned a handful of tobacco plantations along the James River and probably earned a good living from them. The average grain farmer made about eighteen dollars a year planting wheat; the same land used to grow the more labor intensive tobacco in the new world could make the planter one hundred dollars a year.[1] The magnitude of difference is accounted for by inexpensive slave labor employed to plant, weed, water, cultivate, cut, stem, cure, pack, and transport the leaf. It was nasty, backbreaking work requiring some forty steps during the entire growing season. Forests were flattened and a layer of ash was laid down for the small tobacco seeds to germinate. When the plants grew to four inches, field slaves would transplant them into a larger growing area, setting them in rows four feet apart. A single slave crew might be responsible for 20,000 plants; they would spend hours weeding and searching for hornworms, whose giant caterpillarlike bodies inflated with green fluid as they sucked nutrients from the plant. When the buds arrived a month later, the plants were pruned; in another six weeks the leaves would be harvested, then dried in a curing barn.

The leaves would be jammed into wooden barrels called hogsheads. "A barefoot slave stood inside the barrel and layered the 'hands,' packing the tobacco tight with the aid of blocks and levers before 'heading' (putting the lid onto) the hogshead. When the shipment was ready, slaves rolled, carted, or transported the 500-to-1,300-pound hogsheads by boat to the planter's wharf."[2]

A field of tobacco can deplete the soil of its nutrients in as little as three growing seasons. In those early years the Falwells would have lived a nomadic life. It's what drove early immigrants west, founding settlements along the James River as the soil was vacuumed of its vitality. The Falwells may have also planted their fields along the routes of deerskin traders who had made the Powhatans business partners. The Powhatans later traded their food crops for tobacco until they watched the colonists expand their plantations into Indian lands, reigniting feuds and causing the need for settlers to once again move on.

About one hundred miles downriver from Jamestown, the James widens and makes a sharp bend from south to west. It's an ideal crossing when the water is low—hunting parties of Monacan Indians, the Powhatans' rivals, once chased galloping buffalo across the river. When the water runs deep, it's a perfect stretch for navigation but is impossible to cross without a boat. A family of Irish immigrants, originally known as the Lichts (who changed their name to a more Anglo-sounding "Lynch" when they came to Ireland from their native France), started a farm and began running a ferry across the river in 1757. In doing so, they created a rich channel of commerce for frontier families who were then arriving on either bank of the James. The man credited with starting this ferry was a tobacco farmer and Quaker named John Lynch.

Lynchburg was officially founded in 1786, after Lynch sold forty-five acres of land to Virginia's general assembly, which incorporated the town within its boundaries. He dodged local taxes by placing his tobacco warehouse just outside city limits.[3] It was a good spot for a ferry, but a maddening place to start a town. Much of Lynchburg's acreage ran along the steep slopes of the James, creating engineering nightmares for home builders. Among these slopes are the city's seven hills, giving rise to its nickname, the Hill City. The name Lynchburg itself is something of a misnomer, given there has never been a lynching here and the fact that Lynch himself emancipated his slaves soon after he settled near the river.

The English divided the Virginia colony into eight gigantic shires, subdivided over the generations into counties. Lynchburg occupies unique geography in that it's surrounded by four counties—Amherst, Appomattox, Bedford, and Campbell—yet its land resides in none of them. By the time of Lynchburg's founding, the fourth- or fifth-generation Falwells had likely made it as far as Buckingham County. Early Lynchburg was a wild little hollow cut into the foothills of the Blue Ridge Mountains. Disputes were settled so often by pistols that the founding members of the city council were forced to sign a pledge that they would not participate in duels while in office.[4] Saloons blossomed; it would be two years before the first official church appeared. Few soon followed, prompting visiting evangelist Lorenzo Dow to remark in 1804 that Lynchburg was "the seat of Satan's kingdom."[5]

The tiny town, with a population of about five hundred, would soon be the center of a flowering industry. Tobacco moguls like John W. Carroll were literally minted overnight. One evening, playing a round of five-card stud, he wound up with three jacks and was dealt a fourth, winning five thousand dollars. He used the money to start his famous "Lone Jack" brand of pipe tobacco.[6]

Lynchburg's tobacco wealth accelerated when planters realized the folly of shipping their crop all the way to Richmond to be processed. Hogsheads had to be loaded onto flat-bottomed bateaux, whose skippers navigated the freight around rocks and punishing rapids. Tobacco farmers started packaging their product themselves, cutting out the middlemen in Richmond. By the late eighteenth century, Virginia was exporting 100 million pounds of processed tobacco a year, much of it directly from Lynchburg.[7]

Thomas Jefferson, himself a tobacco farmer, built a summer home in Poplar Forest on the northwest outskirts of Lynchburg after his term as president. He called Lynchburg "the most interesting spot in the state" and often dined in town on his way to Monticello, some seventy miles to the north in Charlottesville. At the turn of the eighteenth century, Lynchburg was becoming a major trading hub between the territories of the west and the states in the east. In a letter to U.S. Postmaster General Gideon Granger in 1810, Jefferson lauded Lynchburg as the fastest-growing town in the United States, and lobbied for postal deliveries from Richmond to go from once a week to twice a week.[8] Jefferson was so enamored with this small town that he believed Lynchburg would be one of the nation's three main economic crossroads, along with Philadelphia and New York.

The businessmen of Lynchburg showed their affection for Jefferson by trying to bail him out of his impending bankruptcy in 1826. That year Jefferson asked Virginia's general assembly to allow him to hold a lottery to pay off his massive debts. He would offer his three homes, including Monticello, then worth $71,000.[9]

A bill passed granting him that wish. But Lynchburg's business community was horrified that a founding father would be subject to such humiliation. They decided to raise money for Jefferson by subscription. Lottery tickets would also be sold at ten dollars apiece for a drawing in Richmond in October. Jefferson rendered all these ventures moot when he died on July 4, 1826.

Unlike the English, whose cultural elite judged tobacco by the quality of its smoke, Lynchburgers mostly chewed their leaf. Pipes and cigars were common, but smoking cigarettes was almost unheard of. Spittoons could be found in nearly every corner of every town building. Even so, great gobs of dried tobacco spit sat drying on walls and floors. Charles Dickens once visited Virginia and publicly mocked the sight of "yellow streams" of tobacco juice trickling down the chins of its residents. The sentiment sent editorial writers at the town's leading newspaper into a tirade. In 1860, the *Virginian* stated: "We are incensed at the everlasting twaddle of the English in denouncing our own private habit. If a man is ugly, he does not want to be continually told of it." The *Virginian* then equated spitting with patriotism: "We are freemen, and it is one of our inalienable franchises to expectorate. Lynchburgers especially are entitled to indulge in this nationalism. They are in the very midst of the weed upon which the habit subsists; it is their living, their meat and their drink . . . Let us expectorate proudly."[10] That sentiment was nothing to spit at. The tobacco boom had created so much wealth so quickly that Lynchburg had gained the second highest per capita income of any city in the United States. The first was New Bedford, Massachusetts, capital of New England's whaling industry.[11]

This is the Lynchburg that Jerry Falwell's great-grandfather,

Hezekiah Carey Falwell, encountered in 1850, when he traveled by horseback from his tobacco farm in Buckingham County to the outskirts of town. He had made a mint as a farmer and owned a handful of slaves. Now he was looking for a parcel of land big enough to raise dairy cows and stable horses. In 1854, Hezekiah married Emily Bruce, the daughter of George M. Bruce, founder of Virginia's first stagecoach line, which carried passengers between Lynchburg and the Shenandoah Valley. Bruce's partner was Billy Smith, the state's two-time governor and a Confederate general in the Civil War (Smith was hard to miss on the battlefield, known for wearing a tall beaver hat and clutching a blue umbrella).

Hezekiah and his brother John bought 1,500 acres of land on the northeast slopes of what later became Candler's Mountain (rechristened in the 1980s by the Falwells as "Liberty Mountain"). Its well-timbered hills were thick with sweet gum and dogwood trees, meandering creeks, and freshwater springs. The scope of this rolling forest was massive—more than thirty times the city of Lynchburg itself. As the family grew, their businesses multiplied. Some descendants grew corn and hay; others ran dairies and harvested sugarcane and sassafras. Some took parcels of land they inherited and sold them off to tobacco growers, or grew the leaf themselves.

Riches from the tobacco trade unleashed modernizations that insular Lynchburg was unaccustomed to. In the decade Hezekiah arrived, Lynchburg got its first railroad lines, sewer systems, and gaslight lamps. The town was home to three railroads and a canal planned by George Washington. Mansions built by tobacco barons looked down from the city's seven hills. Lynchburg's economy rivaled that of the city of Richmond. In the decade before the start of the Civil War, Lynchburg had suddenly became a cosmopolitan hub of Southern culture.

This rollicking growth ended on May 23, 1861, when all 1,486 of Lynchburg's registered voters (of a population of about 7,000) cast their ballots to secede from the Union.[12] The Falwells did their part for Dixie: Hezekiah Falwell and his family farmed vegetables for Confederate soldiers on his land and stabled officers' horses there. His brother John Falwell fought in the Confederate army. Over the next few years, Virginia, the central battlefield of the Civil War, would suffer 400,000 casualties on its soil. Lynchburg would be transformed from a railroad town to a giant terminus for bleeding, wounded, and dying soldiers—a serious challenge, given the city had no hospitals. Old Lynchburg College, two of Lynchburg's biggest hotels, and most of the town's tobacco warehouses were turned into wards for the sick and wounded. Some 2,500 Confederate troops would die in these makeshift hospitals. That the city survived the entire war virtually untouched is remarkable. Lynchburg was the terminus of the Salem Turnpike, the chief transportation artery through southwest Virginia. In the last months of 1864, the city of Richmond continued to function only because Lynchburg was sending supplies east to the Confederate capital on its railroads, whose cars would return filled with wounded rebel soldiers.

Only once did Lynchburg face serious peril. In June 1864, Union General David Hunter was ordered by Gen. Ulysses S. Grant to destroy the city's rail and river links. On his way to Lynchburg through the Shenandoah Valley, Hunter's troops unleashed a reign of terror, torching homes and farms, culminating with the burning of the Virginia Military Institute at Lexington.

Confederate Gen. Jubal Early arrived in Lynchburg with a handful of troops to drive the Yankees back. He was greatly outnumbered; it would be days before the rest of his forces would arrive. Early moved Lynchburg's lines of defense farther out of town, then devised a clever feint. After dark, he ordered a single switch engine and a few empty cars at the Lynchburg rail station to begin running back and forth. When the train came in its arrival was met with a deafening roar from a crowd as a band played.[13] The cacophony went on all night. Early knew that Hunter's spies would arrive ahead of the Union troops to assess the enemy's strength. The scouts, in fact, reported back to Hunter that they heard trainload after trainload of reinforcements arriving and that the Union troops could well be outnumbered. Hunter was suckered by Early's ruse and retreated by way of Buford's Gap into the Blue Ridge Mountains.

Lynchburg was saved, but as the Union armies converged on central Virginia, courthouses and city archives were burned and destroyed. Troves of genealogical records were lost, including thousands of marriage certificates, deeds, and birth records. There are thirty-nine "burned record counties" in Virginia, grouped by "hopeless," "almost hopeless," and "difficult." Much of the Falwell family records fall into the "hopeless" category, though not solely from Civil War losses. In 1869, a spiteful tenant farmer in the midst of a property dispute burned down the Buckingham County courthouse. He succeeded in erasing the legal records of his landlord, but also incinerated three generations of Falwell family history.

One tenuous link between the Falwells and the Civil War remains: the legend of the Beale Treasure. In 1885, a twenty-three-page booklet titled *The Beale Papers* went on sale in Lynchburg for fifty cents per copy. The document, published by James B. Ward, told the tale of a hunting party which, in the course of chasing a herd of buffalo in northern New Mexico, stumbled upon a massive out-cropping of gold and silver in a ravine. They mined two tons of the precious metals and deposited their mother lode in Bedford County, Virginia, in 1819 and 1821. The treasure safely hidden, Thomas J. Beale, who led the party, returned to the west for a final prospecting trip. Whether Beale and his party were killed by Indians or outlaws is unknown, but they never returned. The value today of this fortune would be about $40 million.

Beale apparently recognized the dangers of a second voyage. So he gave a Bedford innkeeper he knew and trusted, Robert Morriss, a small iron box containing three cipher cryptograms stating the location of an underground vault that held the treasure. Beale did not reveal the contents of the box, but instructed Morriss to wait for a letter (which contained the keys) from Beale, which would explain its contents. Beale further instructed that if he did not return in ten years' time, then Morriss should open the box. The keys never arrived, and Beale never returned. Some years later Morriss finally opened the box and discovered the pages of code. He made no headway deciphering the messages. Exasperated, he gave the letters to Ward, who broke one of the code sheets using the Declaration of Independence as the key. It describes the treasure in detail. But Ward was unsuccessful in cracking the other two cryptograms, which contained names of those who held claim to the fortune and where it was buried. He decided to publish them.

Since then, graves have been dug up and apple orchards excavated all over Bedford County, just west of Lynchburg. Psychics, mathematicians, and cryptographers at the National Security Agency have tried to crack the codes. A new theory emerged some years ago, alleging that the Beale hoard was actually the Confederate treasury, smuggled out of Richmond and buried in Lynchburg as the capital burned in 1865. The Beale tale was just a cover story, the theory goes, concocted by those who wanted to protect the loot until the South could rise again. Ferdinand C. Hutter, Ward's cousin, was a Confederate paymaster in 1865 (he cut Robert E. Lee his first check) when he fled Richmond. Hutter lived in the house Jerry Falwell lived in until his death. This fact has fueled the theory that the *Beale Papers* were actually drafted by Hutter, and that the Confederate treasury lies buried at the Falwell home. "Jerry loved to joke about it," says Beale treasure authority Peter Viemeister. "But I don't think he believed it."

Lynchburg's tobacco economy never quite recovered from the Civil War, but its modern transportation hubs made it an attractive locale for foundries and machine works, cotton mills, and a handful of colleges. Among the new companies that came into town: Craddock-Terry Shoe Co., the largest maker of shoes in the South, and pharmaceutical maker C. B. Fleet. In the 1950s, what author Darrell Laurant calls "The Second Northern Invasion" juiced Lynchburg's economy with the addition of a colossal General Electric mobile-communications facility and a Babcock & Wilcox nuclear power plant five miles from town.

Jerry Falwell grew up in this economic boomlet and would start a church, which would grow to 22,000 in a town of 64,000. He has long been considered Lynchburg's most influential citizen, but only by those who have forgotten the name Carter Glass.

Glass invented the Federal Reserve and authored the most

sweeping banking reforms in American history. His climb to power began in 1888, when he bought one of Lynchburg's biggest dailies, *The Lynchburg News*. A few years later his father, Robert Glass, took over as editor of its rival, the *Advance*. A father-son newspaper war erupted until *The News*, having bought a handful of other papers, finally swallowed the *Advance*. For the next three decades, Carter Glass would control Lynchburg's only major newspaper.

Glass was elected to the Virginia Senate in 1899, and won a seat in the U.S. House in 1902. Woodrow Wilson named Glass secretary of the treasury in 1919. That post also made Glass the top antiliquor enforcement officer during Prohibition. He was undoubtedly aware that one of the biggest bootleggers in Virginia—Carey Farwell—lived and worked just a few miles from Glass's hilltop mansion. Yet, he may also thought it unwise to mess with Carey, given half of Lynchburg's police force were his customers, including the chief of police.

Glass lived in a two-story brick cottage on a hill overlooking a grazing pasture for his Jersey cows. The cottage is built with timber from Glass's earlier home on the same site, where Glass composed drafts of the Federal Reserve Act. Glass would have been stunned to learn that his cow pasture would one day become the center of a fundamentalist Christian university started by Carey's son, Jerry.

Glass waited until the tender young age of seventy-five to deliver his second and final act: the Glass-Steagall bill of 1933. Its purpose was to stamp out conflicts of interest at commercial banks who underwrote securities. It separated commercial and investment banking and allowed use of U.S. government securities as collateral for Federal Reserve notes. The act remained in force for seven decades before it was repealed in 1999. Up until then, anyone possessing a $50,000 Treasury bill would know Glass's face—his likeness appeared on the left-hand side of the note. Glass made his final appearance on the bill in 1997, the year the last one matured (they are no longer printed on paper).

A careful stock watcher, Glass was probably astonished to find that on the day of the stock-market crash, his own paper, *The News,* ran the story of the collapse on the inside. If the crash of the U.S. stock market didn't make page one, what did? There, beginning in the left-hand column, was a two-page account of a wild shootout between two brothers at a gas station. The first sentence of the story got right to the point: "Garland Falwell is dead."

2. Verbal Vigilantes

EZEKIAH Falwell was only fifty-nine when he died in 1886, the year his seven children divvied up the massive acreage he controlled on Candler's Mountain. Among them was a son, Charles William Falwell, who grew sugarcane to make blackstrap molasses and had started the Meadow View dairy, selling milk for three cents a quart, which he delivered by horse-drawn wagon. Lynchburg was rife with dairies, including Carter Glass's Montview farm on the other side of the mountain. Charlie's land was contiguous to the land of his siblings. "They didn't have telephones, so when a message came along, they'd relay it farm to farm by hollerin' at the top of their lungs," cracked Edna "Peewee" Twitty, Charlie's granddaughter. A horseback ride from one end of the Falwell properties to the other might take an hour. Charlie's four sons figured out faster means of conveyance; most of the businesses they constructed in the early 1900s were built around motorized transportation.

Charlie's second oldest son, Carey, was born in 1893. He stood six feet tall, with a broad, lined forehead, a dour smile, piercing brown eyes, callused fingers, and big-boned hands. Folks around town knew he carried a gun; exactly why was unclear. Carey's wife, Helen Beasley, grew up in a 100-person town called Hollywood, near Appomattox. Her ancestors were wealthy, tobacco-growing Baptists. The family plantation was decimated during the Civil War, and Helen grew up dirt poor. She and her fifteen brothers and sisters worked on the family tobacco farm themselves. Her parents would give her a penny for every hundred hornworms she picked off the young tobacco stalks. Before Sunday service she and her brothers and sisters took turns bathing in a single tin bathtub.

In his teens Carey found work as a security agent for the Burns Detective Agency in Roanoke; in his twenties, during World War I, he was hired by the Norfolk and Western Railroad to watch Campbell County bridges on the James River. The only lawlessness he encountered was a thief stealing coal from a railcar. Carey shot and wounded the perpetrator as he tried to flee. Guard duty watching bridges kept him out of combat during the war and helped him save seed money to open the C. H. Falwell Grocery and General Store in 1915. He stocked it with chicken feed, lard, baloney sausage, hay, chestnuts, and livermush, a Southern version of scrapple.

Lynchburg was a small town in central Virginia, but even here it was obvious that the automobile was putting an end to the era of Uncle Charlie's horse-drawn carriage. Carey used his store as collateral for a loan from a local bank to open a handful of Quaker

State oil franchises. Low start-up costs helped him generate cash flow in no time. Carey sold his lender on the notion that he could expand his customer base by adding filling stations to his franchise territory. His banker agreed, giving Carey a series of loans to buy or build seventeen filling stations in town, including one in front of his own home on Old Rustburg Road. He hauled a pair of fuel tanks to a clearing just above his house, where a refinery truck would drive to the tanks and unload gas. Using gravity for propulsion, Carey drew the fuel through pipes past his home and down to a pump tank at the filling station he had built beside the road. The structure stands today in front of the house where Gene Falwell, Jerry Falwell's fraternal twin, still lives with his wife Joanne.

The new car culture sent demand for fuel soaring in the 1920s, turning Carey into the Leon Hess of Lynchburg. Plenty of people didn't yet own autos—Carey went after that market, too. He started a passenger-bus company with his brother Warren, who ran a thirty-four-car taxi fleet in Lynchburg. They called it the American Bus Lines and made stops in Washington, D.C., Durham, North Carolina, and Lexington, Virginia. Carey had no accounting experience, but kept meticulous records. He scribbled away on thick ledgers, detailing the ebb and flow of passenger volume on his rigs. He tracked demand for fuel at his filling stations to the gallon and was constantly haggling with suppliers for cheaper volume discounts on the "white lightning" he procured from illegal hooch makers.

The earnings from his liquor, fuel, and restaurant businesses vaunted Carey into Lynchburg's wealthy class. His home, on seven acres, had apple and oak trees, a smokehouse, a slaughterhouse, and chicken coops. Times were so good that when Jerry and Gene were old enough Carey sent them to elementary school with a car and driver. But Carey's newfound wealth did not stop him from loathing the carpetbagging first-generation Lynchburgers who profited from the Reconstruction economy. They walked about town in top hats and lived in the splendid Tudor and Georgian mansions built by Lynchburg's tobacco barons atop the city's seven hills. Some of the members of Lynchburg's nouveau riche had attended fine schools back east; Carey never made it past sixth grade. They were Republicans; Carey was an FDR Democrat. Most were Methodists, Baptists, or Catholics. He was an agnostic who rarely went near a church.

Carey didn't care for the local church pastors, either. He once warned his son Lewis never to trust a priest, much less become one. "When a preacher walks into a room, people start actin' funny."[1] Carey only rarely tolerated the presence of God in his home. The family did not say grace before dinner or pray together. The only nod to religion Carey made was to let Helen, a devout Baptist, take son Lewis and daughter Rosha to church on Sunday.

Carey was even stricter with his own employees. He practiced a brand of workplace discipline that would make an OSHA inspector cringe. There's the story of Crip Smith, a one-legged employee of Carey's oil company who never seemed to tire of complaining about long hours. One day Smith called in sick. Carey and some friends went out to Smith's house, trapped his black tomcat, killed the creature, and cooked its innards at one of Carey's restaurants. The remains were daintily plated upon a linen covered platter and sent over to Smith's home with a get-well note, describing the dish as a complimentary lunch of roast squirrel. The next day, back at work, Smith was complaining again, this time about how he had never tasted such chewy meat. Carey was apparently only too happy to tell Smith the origins of his meal.[2] Carey's malicious pranks weren't only reserved for employees. He loved scaring the devil out of friends and family. He once shot a hole through the floor of his own kitchen, pretending to be aiming for a fly just to mortify a friend of his son Jerry, then twelve years old; the friend never set foot in the Falwell home again.[3]

Carey's best business years were the mid-1930s, at the birth of the swing era, when he built the Merry Garden Dance Hall on a hilltop just east of Lynchburg, part of Hezekiah's original parcel. Its 10,000-square-foot main hall was the biggest for miles around and seated one thousand guests for dinner. He charged a one-dollar cover. You could get a banana salad for twenty-five cents; wine for $1.50 per quart. Waiters dressed in formal wear, and the tables were set with china. Carey put his restaurant to less formal uses, too. He hosted comedy acts, traveling circuses, and magicians. Tommy Dorsey and his band headlined one weekend.

Nearby, on another hilltop, Carey opened a restaurant and hotel called the Old Fort Inn. It was a cluster of thirty-two cottages overlooking the city, with showers, steam heat, a swimming pool, and round-the-clock room service. The Old Fort was one of the first hotels in the area to offer such swanky amenities, and certainly the only establishment with a cage outside containing a 200-pound black bear named Gertie. The critter was owned by Carey, who'd occasionally take the beast for a swim in his hotel's swimming pool and out for walks, shocking tourists, who bolted for their cameras at the sight. A sign on the cage offered a fifty-dollar prize to anyone who could "throw" Gertie. According to family lore, one afternoon a drunken customer turned rambunctious in the Old Fort's dining room, threatening that he could beat up anyone in the restaurant. Carey responded by grabbing the man and pulling him outside, yelling as he pointed to Gertie, "You want to fight? Fight him!" Carey hauled the offender into the cage. By the time he let the customer out he was mauled, but still breathing.[4]

Carey controlled most of Lynchburg's fuel supply and a large share of its liquor distribution. "Lynchburg was like Little Chicago," says Lynchburg history docent Vince Desmond. "If you wanted gas or booze, you had to buy it through Carey." Carey's businesses flourished in the early 1930s, but he didn't seem to enjoy his success much. The deaths of two family members overwhelmed him. The first was Carey's daughter, ten-year-old Rosha Falwell, who died of peritonitus after her appendix burst in 1931. Six months later Carey shot Garland to death. His guilt over the shooting became a daily, horrific preoccupation. He began submerging his chronic self-recriminations in alcohol. Carey thought nothing of downing a dozen whiskies through the late afternoon and evening, each one chased by a beer.

At home on Rustburg Road, Carey typically awoke before dawn and ambled into the kitchen, where he sat quietly sipping a cup of Helen's potent coffee. He loved the quiet; it gave him relief from his pounding head, the result of his late-night boozing. Helen was always up before him, setting the morning table as fried eggs and fatback bacon sizzled in cast-iron skillets next to a pot of sausage gravy. There was a wood-burning stove in the corner near the chiller, where Carey deposited a fifty-pound block of ice each week. Carey silently munched hoecakes drenched in the gravy as he pored through the morning edition of *The News*. He checked the latest grain prices and marveled at the technological advancements

of the day. At that time, *The News's* pages often carried advertisements for prepackaged sliced bread, an innovation that would end
"torn crusts and knife injuries" once and for all. There was once a
story from Paris about an early form of instant messaging: At a
restaurant in Montmartre, "Telephones have been installed at each
of the tables so that diners may converse with each other across
the room. The big dollars and cents man from Indiana who never
would dare walk over and ask the pretty blonde for a dance now
can converse over a telephone with semi privacy."[5] Progress indeed.

After breakfast Carey buttoned up the jacket of his brown,
double-breasted suit and placed a tall, snug-fitting brown felt hat
atop his head. Its front brim, tilted down on his forehead, gave him
the look of a homicide detective. Inside his right vest pocket was a
gold railroad pocket watch. Beneath his left arm he tucked a pearl-
handled .38 Remington into a holster. The gun was never far from
reach.

In 1933, Helen gave birth to twin boys, Jerry and Gene. They
were both named for their late sister Rosha, whose middle name
was Geraldine. Their father looked in on the boys in the morning,
but he was always gone before they rose. Carey hired a one-eyed
African American man named David Brown to help care for Jerry
and Gene. Brown bathed and dressed the twins, and played with
them in a meadow near the Falwells' home.[6] The twins buoyed
Carey's spirits for a while.

The Depression was taking its toll on Carey's businesses, starting with the Merry Garden, whose typically stable flow of evening
events and big dinner parties had slowed to a trickle. The catering
side of his business, where most of his restaurant's money was
made, was hit hard. A second blow to Carey's enterprises came a

few years later with the end of Prohibition. The ubiquitous "nip joints," fueled by Carey's booze, began to dry up. His bootlegging income collapsed. In 1942, the federal government would order fuel rationing, limiting drivers to using three gallons a week. Carey's chain of filling stations felt the effects; he was soon forced to sell them. To keep himself and his family alive, Carey sold dirt, firewood, and coal out of his barn, where he moved his office. The handbills he distributed to customers carried an air of desperation: "Call me day or night."

It was a staggering fall from grace. Having been one of Lynchburg's most powerful businessmen, he now sold what he called "rich dirt," soil mixed with lime, for three dollars per shovelful. He was forced to sell the Merry Garden to his brother Warren, who turned it into a roller rink. About all that remained was a chest full of life insurance policies he had purchased over the years. "Carey had more life insurance taken out on himself than any other man in the state of Virginia," recalls Gene Falwell.

Jerry Falwell's father had used dozens of loans and other forms of financial leverage to build his companies, but could not find a way to leverage himself out his financial wipeout. His heavy drinking didn't help; it turned him short-fused and irritable. He fell into drunken rages at night, taking his frustrations out on poor David Brown, whom Helen would always defend. Carey then turned on her, exploding: "Helen, you're nothing but a goddamn nigger lover!"[7]

Carey Falwell's home on Rustburg Road was becoming an open bar. Whiskey flasks sat in the living room and half-filled glasses of bourbon littered the house. Crates of beer were stacked on the porch; barrels of wine sat in the basement. His descent into alcoholism shocked even his oldest friends. They sat with him into the late hours in his barn. Carey's liquor, gas, and restaurant enterprises lay in tatters, yet strangely, his preoccupation was not his financial morass, but the circumstances of the night he killed Garland. Carey stayed up late evenings with son-in-law Lawrence Jennings, who didn't drink much, but was a good listener. Carey explained he hadn't really killed Garland. "He killed himself, you know." Then, with a desperate look in his eyes, Carey would stare at Lawrence, and say, "If you ever have to kill anybody, kill yourself instead."[8]

Gene was in denial over his father's drinking, learning the mechanic's trade and spending much of his time disassembling tractor engines at a friend's gas station. But thirteen-year-old Jerry was becoming profoundly disturbed by his dad's constant boozing. Jerry was growing into an articulate, precociously clever kid. These were his father's qualities. Now Carey's agile mental reflexes were gumming up like molasses; his speech sometimes slurred, the piercing brown eyes unfocused. The central figure in Jerry Falwell's life was disintegrating. Jerry felt guilty, as if he and Gene were doing something to drive their father away. Jerry's rational mind kept dismissing the thought, but deep down he felt somehow responsible. It is irrational guilt commonly felt among children of alcoholics. Why else would a parent seek to escape from the reality they share with their kids, unless the kids were doing something to drive them away?

Late one night Jerry discovered his father unconscious in a field between the barn and the Falwell home. In the light of a half-moon, he could see his father sprawled on his side, mouth agape, coins scattered on the ground beside him where they had tumbled from his pocket. It was an awful sight. Jerry knelt next to Carey and pulled him to his feet, the stench of bourbon thick on his breath. Groggy and disoriented, Carey walked slowly, silently, with his son to the back door of their home. Jerry could feel Carey's stooped posture; his father suddenly resembled an old man. Carey sat down, stupefied.[9] His father said nothing, but Jerry knew that he had spent yet another evening agonizing over Garland's death.

Later that year Carey's abdomen began to swell, his face became puffy, and he battled intense fatigue, languishing in bed for hours. His skin took on a yellow tone, and fluid began collecting around his abdomen. He was soon diagnosed with cirrhosis. Even so, he remained wary of hospitals and refused to visit one, still believing they failed to save his daughter Rosha. Doctors who came to see him didn't give him much time. After prodding from a close friend, Carey agreed to a sickbed conversion to Christ. A local pastor helped Carey make a prayer of confession. What Carey confessed is unknown; he swore the pastor to secrecy. On an October evening in 1948, Carey caught pneumonia and died the next day. His sons, Jerry and Gene, were just fifteen.

Jerry Falwell spoke often of his own religious conversion, which occurred four years later. But it is this earlier point in time—the moment of his father's passing—that marks the real beginning of Falwell's religious journey. When Falwell's father died, an oppressive veil lifted around Helen's passion for sharing her Christian faith. There had been a bitter tension between his mother's vibrant spirituality and his father's pugnacious hostility to it. Helen could now freely share her Baptist beliefs with her four children unhindered by her Godless husband. Carey was liberated, too. The searing, unresolved guilt that plagued him for seventeen years was finally gone.

J ERRY Falwell's first job wasn't selling faith, but fish. In the spring of 1945, he and Gene got the idea to peddle mud kittens (baby catfish) and minnows from a wooden bait stand in front of the family home on Rustburg Road. Like so many of Falwell's future enterprises, the venture was backed by a loyal benefactor—his father—who put his boys in the care of one of his fuel oil truck drivers to help collect the merchandise. The trio drove out to some of the larger creeks, where they dropped nets into the water, skimming the bottom, then selling their squirming catch to fishermen on their way to the James River. For four fishing seasons they sold minnows at fifty cents a dozen, mud kittens for $1.25 a dozen, plus snails, earthworms, and crickets, making as much as fifty dollars a day. "We sold anything that moved," recalled Gene.

In his teenage years Falwell began attending church, but only to hunt for dates among the array of pretty blonde and brunette teenage girls in attendance. He hung out with a band of juvenile delinquents known as the Wall Gang, so named for a retaining wall where they would gather at after dark. Falwell was the gang's "president." He led attacks on rival gangs at the local roller rink, the scene of dozens of intergang clashes. Numbering about forty kids, Falwell's followers spent their Sunday evenings drinking beer at the wall, hollering and singing late into the night. A neighbor once called the police about the noise. The gang wreaked revenge, Garland Falwell style.

A group of them, Falwell included, found a pile of railroad ties sitting in a pool of tar. They piled the ties in front of the home of the complaining neighbor, poured several gallons of gasoline on the sticky mess, then set it aflame. But they had used too much fuel. The ties ignited like a bonfire, then a wall of flame raced in either direction along the road. Falwell and his friends had set a fire running nearly the entire length of the block.[10] They fled like the wind as fire trucks and police arrived. Miraculously, no one died. The occupants of the house in front of which the fire had started were not known to have complained again.

At the time of his father's death, Falwell was a junior at Brookville High School. Like all schools in Virginia at the time, Brookville was segregated. Jerry and Gene would arrive each day just in time to see an old black janitor named Marshall raising the American flag. "Morning, Mr. Jerry," he'd say to Falwell as he and Gene arrived. Some days the brothers would join Marshall for lunch down in the school's furnace room.[11]

Falwell was seventeen in his first year at Lynchburg College; he had been moved ahead a grade. He earned straight-A's and turned into an overachieving jock. On the football squad he played fullback on offense, safety on defense. On the baseball team he played left field. A scout from the farm team for the St. Louis Cardinals asked Falwell to try out for a spot; he clinched it. As strong as his academics and athletics were, he felt ambiguous about career plans. He was considering attending Virginia Tech for an engineering degree, but was also thinking about a journalism career. He didn't like the idea of leaving Lynchburg; that was something Falwells just didn't do. But he didn't relish working in any of the remaining family businesses, either.

When Falwell and his brother Gene came to the breakfast table on Sundays his mother Helen would turn up on the radio the *Old Fashioned Revival Hour* to an earsplitting volume. The show was hosted by fundamentalist Baptist minister Charles E. Fuller, the man responsible for the Big Bang of electronic evangelism. A former California orange grower, Fuller started a Christian radio ministry above a shoe store in Long Beach, assembling a radio network of 525 stations in the 1930s. Twenty years later, Fuller was broadcast on one thousand stations, uniting conservative Protestants coast to coast. His show was listened to by miners in Ohio, sheepherders in North Dakota, and prisoners at San Quentin.

Fuller's program wasn't a church service but a one-hour music show and sermon backed by a sonorous quartet. As Falwell sat eating his ham and hoecakes he listened to Fuller's booming voice, imagining a Christian Zeus heaving theological thunderbolts at enemies. His father had told him that preachers were weak and insincere. Not Fuller. In fact, the power of Fuller's blistering rhetoric reminded him of the intimidating presence of his father before he descended into alcoholic oblivion. In Carey's last days God had made his father strong again. He felt that strength in Fuller's voice. As the months rolled by, Falwell began looking up to the unseen man behind the voice almost as a surrogate father. To Falwell, Fuller was a rock star with audacious charisma. Falwell daydreamed what it would be like to see him in person.

One night, hanging out with his Wall Gang pals, he asked someone whether they knew of a church in Lynchburg with Fuller's brand of Christian fire. There was one: the Park Avenue Baptist Church. It even used Fuller's songbooks. Could a church that followed Fuller's philosophy possess the excitement Fuller conveyed over radio? Even if it didn't, there would be a consolation prize: Park Avenue was known to be frequented by some of the loveliest teenage girls in Lynchburg.

Falwell finally convinced two members of the Wall Gang, Jim Moon and Otis Wright, to accompany him to the Park Avenue church one evening. It was January 20, 1952. When the trio showed up at the cinder-block building, Falwell's cohorts imagined he was up to a prank. They were seated in the church's front row, where they immediately fixed their gaze on two young female pianists on either end of the stage. The girls banged out accompaniment to a small choir that was singing, "The win-dows of hea-a-ven are open. The bless-ings are flowing to-night."[12] Moon turned to Falwell and, pointing to one of the pianists, a slender brunette named Macel Pate, yelled, "I'm going to ask her out. Whadda think?" Falwell nodded, then pointed to the other pianist, Dolores Hart, and smiled. "Okay, that one's mine." Then Falwell looked back at Macel, wishing he had claimed her first.

As the evening wore on, Falwell felt strangely at home with the singing and the preaching. Fuller's radio show had come to life. Most of the congregation was young, including its self-assured, twenty-nine-year-old pastor, Paul Donnelson. Near the end of the service a wrinkled old gent asked Falwell if he wanted to approach the altar. Falwell agreed, and knelt down. The man began reading from the book of Romans, explaining what it meant to be saved. Falwell closed his eyes, concentrating on the words. His mind raced back to the last memory he had of his father. Carey was in bed, smiling, having just given himself to God. Falwell felt his father's presence and realized that what Carey had found at the end of his life, he was discovering at the beginning of his. Falwell agreed to be saved.

In the days following his conversion, he rode a wave of manic euphoria. Was it the thrill of finding God—or finding love? Or both? Macel, the pianist, was becoming his obsession. "Macel's smile made me weak. Her lips were perfectly bowed. She had dimples and a tiny bobbed nose. Her blue eyes sparkled when she played and her slender shoulders swayed gently with the music," said Falwell. But Macel was engaged to a young man who was neck deep in religious studies at a Bible school in Springfield, Missouri. Macel kept her distance from Falwell; she knew he was the ringleader of the Wall Gang and came from a family with a vulgar past. It did little to deter her suitor. When he arrived at church, he placed his folding chair as close to Macel as possible. He wanted to ask her out for a date, but settled for the next best thing: accompanying her on witnessing missions around town.

Just two months after his first visit to the Park Avenue church, his advances were gaining ground. At a music rehearsal in the church basement, Macel arrived and found herself without a piano bench. The chair left behind to replace it was too low. Falwell offered to sit in the chair, and told Macel to sit on his lap. Macel complied. "I kept my hands at my side and tried to look cool and casual. But my heart was beating fast and I wanted to hold her in my arms," remembered Falwell.[13] It was a randy indiscretion, especially at an orthodox church like Park Avenue. Macel knew it put her in a bad light and scolded Falwell for the stunt. After that, for a while, she became cool and aloof. It just made him want her more, of course.

Falwell was also developing lust in his heart for something he had never before considered: leading a church. The idea had come to him as he thought about winning over Macel. There could be no better way to worship God than to start a congregation, and no better reason to stay in Lynchburg, a town where everyone knew his name. There was another reason the idea made sense, though he did not like to think about it or really seek to understand it.

For all his athletic and academic abilities, Jerry Falwell suffered from an inferiority complex rooted in the class resentment that had simmered in his father. Falwell knew people feared Carey, but the elite of Lynchburg did not respect him. In Jerry Falwell's mind, Lynchburg's upper crust dismissed his father as a thug in a suit, a bumpkin who got lucky making a pile off booze and transportation, then lost it all and became a drunkard. Falwell knew he had grown up on the wrong side of town, but his father was no bumpkin, and neither was he. Hadn't he been taken to school by a car and driver? Hadn't his family ridden out the Depression in luxury, while most of the rest of Virginia, and the country, stood in breadlines? Falwell knew he was smarter than most of the bankers, doctors, and lawyers downtown. Starting a church would be a chance to prove it. It would be easier than leading the Wall Gang, he theorized. Church folks tended not to drink and get into fights. Nor did they set fires.

As he looked at the world through a biblical lens, he found a purposefulness to things. His father's alcoholic misery was a battle with Satan. Garland's shooting had the moral pedagogy of Cain and Abel. He believed it was no coincidence that the man who led him to the altar to be converted was a deacon by the name of Garland Carey.

On the advice of Park Avenue pastor Paul Donnelson, Falwell enrolled in Baptist Bible College (BBC), a tiny, unaccredited new school that Macel's fiancé was attending. Falwell was one of the few students with a car, so the school dispatched him as its taxi driver to pick up pastors who came into St. Louis to speak at the BBC. He'd meet and chauffeur some of the old lions of fundamentalism. Like a spiritual Wall Gang, many of them shared Falwell's radical upbringing. There was Dr. John Rawlings, now ninety-four, who lived a hardscrabble childhood in the mountains of Arkansas. "My daddy once shot a man for stealing his corn," he said blithely, as if it were an everyday occurance.

The first time nineteen-year-old Falwell heard him speak, he was enraptured. Rawlings preached about a fight he was in with an Ohio state court. A judge had ordered him to reinstate a member of his church in Cincinnati whom he had expelled. Rawlings was livid. "Our religious liberties are at stake. But will we surrender? NO!" he boomed. "Hell will freeze over before the courts replace God's word as the ultimate, final, and only authority in this place. We will obey God and no other!" Rawlings went on for an hour. His edge-of-the-seat delivery sent chills up Falwell's spine. He wished his father could see the fire coming from Rawlings's tongue. It was a rhetorical Fourth of July.

Falwell's roommate in Springfield turned out to be Julius Blaz, the strapping young man engaged to Macel Pate. Macel was losing interest in Blaz, in part because she never received any letters from him. That's because Falwell, who had kindly offered to drop them at the post office, secretly threw them away. Macel received Falwell's letters instead, and their correspondence soon reflected some serious flirtation.

Falwell chose to study fundamentalism for two reasons: his idol Charles Fuller preached it, and all his friends in church believed in it. It is a macho brand of Christianity, uncompromising and unapologetic—the Christian equivalent of faith on the wrong side of the tracks. Its core belief is that every word in all sixty-six books of the Bible is inspired by God, and therefore "inerrant." The infallible nature of the Bible should be the basis for all history, science, psychology, geography, marriage, friendship, all of Christian history, and every aspect of the human condition. On the matter of the resurrection of Christ, for example, liberal theologians taught that it could be interpreted metaphorically, or entirely as parable. Fundamentalists considered such intellectual flexibility preposterous. If the Bible isn't the literal word of God, they charge, then anything within its pages can be debated.

The champions of fundamentalism were preachers whose names are more reminiscent of wrestling than religion: J. Frank "Texas Tornado" Norris, Robert T. "Fighting Bob" Ketcham, and John L. "Sin Killer" Griffin. They published their views on Christian orthodoxy in periodicals like *Conflict, Dynamite,* and *Sword of the Lord.* They were the most visible promoters of the faith. Yet, fundamentalism's spread probably owes a bigger debt not to any of these fire-breathing pastors, but to a mild-mannered, wealthy oil man named Lyman Stewart.

Stewart was the founder and first president of Union Oil (now Unocal); a Pennsylvania wildcatter who made and lost his first million before he turned forty. A passionate Christian, he bankrolled the publishing of a series of volumes called *The Fundamentals: A Testimony to the Truth.* Several million of these tomes were distributed to priests, pastors, and Sunday-school teachers from 1910 to 1915. They were authored by writers across denominations in North America. Their work remains the very underpinning of the fundamentalist movement.

Fundamentalists felt they needed such a tract because Protestants were beginning to warm to Darwinism and modern science. Symposiums at the Bible Institute in Los Angeles, using *The Fundamentals,* were organized to fight the growing acceptance of vices like liquor, dance halls, and women's suffrage. Rather than galvanizing the faith, these sessions produced a split. "Instead of staying in the major denominations and fighting against the liberals for control, the early fundamentalists withdrew and began their own organizations," explains former Falwell aide Ed Dobson. A few years later fundamentalism suffered an embarrassing defeat at the 1925 Scopes trial. Although biology teacher John T. Scopes was convicted of teaching evolution, the nationwide coverage of the trial depicted fundamentalists as backward, closed-minded zealots. The movement's reputation had been savaged. Fundamentalists turned away from the larger culture.

Falwell enrolled in the BBC just as fundamentalism was reemerging twenty years later, spurred on by the rise of radio preaching. In Springfield, Falwell learned that the Protestant intellectual spectrum consisted of theological liberals on the left, evangelicals in the middle, and fundamentalists on the right.

In his days at Springfield, Falwell kept a Scofield Reference Bible by his side. First published in 1909, its annotated commentary within the text of scripture by Cyrus I. Scofield is a kind of Cliffs Notes for the Gospel. Scofield cross-references themes and dates events such as Creation, which it calculates as occurring in the year 4004 BC. Scofield also advances the nineteenth-century concept of dispensationalism, which holds that all of human history is divided into seven periods, or dispensations, each marking a different way in which God deals with man. Falwell was fascinated by the concept. He came to accept another Scofield precept, premillennialism. This is the belief that Christ will return to "rapture" away the saints before the prophesized seven years of tribulation on earth. The saints will be returned to earth for Christ's thousand-year reign; after that, Christ will battle Satan again and consign him to hell for eternity, followed by a Final Judgment, where every person on earth will either go to heaven or hell.

Near the end of his first year at the BBC, Falwell got a call from Frank Wood, who had replaced Paul Donnelson, Park Avenue's charismatic young pastor. Would Falwell be interested in taking a year off to be youth director? Of course. Wood called John Rawlings to see whether he concurred with his choice of Falwell. "I told him it was probably a bad idea," said Rawlings. "I explained to him the truth, which is that Falwell was smarter than him and sooner or later there'd be trouble." It would be sooner.

Falwell served a year as youth pastor, counseling younger members of the church and helping Wood with administrative tasks. He loved the job but had to resume his studies in Springfield the following year. Some months later he got some astounding news: the Park Avenue church was in the midst of an uprising among its members. A group of them were rebelling against Wood, a meek micromanager who preferred reading his sermons to preaching them. "Wood was used to doing things his own way and didn't like taking suggestions from elder members of the church board," said Falwell childhood friend Jim Moon. So thin-skinned was Wood that rather than tolerate criticism of himself, he held a "no confidence" vote among his three hundred congregants, asking whether he should stay or go. Only about thirty-five voted for him to go. Then Pastor Wood settled the score. He sent "letters of dismissal" to the thirty-five members who defied him, including Macel and Jim Moon's parents.

Having been cast out of their own church, the group of thirty-five decided to form their own congregation. Just who would be radical enough, or crazy enough, to be their new pastor? Perhaps a soon-to-be minted Bible school grad; a Lynchburg native who was known for his own troubled history. A delegation from the group met Falwell in Richmond one day, where he was guest preaching at a small church, and popped the question. The prospect made Falwell's heart pound but filled him with momentary self-doubt. *Who was he, twenty-two-year-old Jerry Falwell, to head up a group of rogue parishoners?* Besides, he had promised friends to pastor a small church in Macon, Georgia. On the other hand, the thought that some upstart preacher had thrown his girlfriend Macel out of her own church made his blood boil.

The split would be more than frowned upon by the Baptist Bible Fellowship, the association of Baptist churches who sanctioned the life and death of new congregations. But the chance to be reunited with Macel overwhelmed him. And, it would fulfill his secret dream of starting his own congregation in his own hometown. An official from the Baptist fellowship called Falwell and urged him not to take the job; if he did, he'd be blacklisted from ever again pastoring at another Baptist church. "Jerry's teachers and peers ostracized him," said Moon. "The whole Baptist establishment turned against him." But could the grassroots passion of Lynchburg churchgoers really be extinguished long distance from a church office in Springfield, Missouri? Falwell thought not. He felt a kind of heady elation when he imagined himself the leader of these troublemakers.

After Falwell offered his acceptance, he drove around town in search of a meeting place and, on a rainy night, discovered an abandoned bottling plant on Thomas Road. The 30-by-50-foot building, surrounded by overgrown weeds, had been the production center for Disney-licensed Donald Duck Soda. The space was filthy, filled with cracked windows, broken floor planks, and sticky black cola syrup dried onto the walls like varnish. It was a depressing, humbling space. But it would work, he thought. His larger problem was the size of his following. There would be $300 in monthly rent to pay; he would need a piano, pews, a pulpit, hymnbooks, and Bibles. Even generous tithing from thirty-five people could only go so far. He remembered a quote from the work of a Baptist church builder he studied in Missouri, W. A. Criswell, who said, "There is nothing wrong with a small church, but there's something wrong with a church that's not growing."[14] Once he started it, how would he expand it?

In spite of the dozens of churches in town, more than half of Lynchburg's then-population of 54,000 was "unchurched." He would find those not yet saved by canvassing every block of the city, house-to-house. If he wound up prying away members of other churches who felt alienated from their own congregations, well, that was fine with him. It was a free-market approach to spirituality. His tactics would be no different than the aggressive, direct selling tactics of, say, an Electrolux vacuum salesman.

Falwell cast himself in slightly more important terms, of course. He sat down in his tiny office inside the former bottling plant, "feeling exactly like Eisenhower as he plotted D-day and the invasion of Europe."[15] He taped a map of Lynchburg to the wall and placed the point of a compass on his Thomas Road location, then drew a circle representing a ten-block radius around the church, imagining it as his personal Jerusalem. He drew another, wider circle encompassing twenty blocks, which he called Judea, ancient home of the Israelites. The next circle he called Samaria, capital of the Kingdom of Israel, and the outlying areas of Lynchburg he labeled "the uttermost parts of the earth."[16]

In those first few weeks of the summer of 1956, in the sticky mountain heat, Falwell put on his best suit, strolled up to strangers' homes and introduced himself and his fledgling church. Then he ran like hell. Falwell confronted barking dogs, guns poking through broken screen doors, and grandmothers furious at having their knitting interrupted. He encountered crotchety shut-ins who didn't cotton to having a loquacious twentysomething leaning on their bell. But for every ten doors that slammed, a mother would stop sweeping and invite him in; a retired millworker would ask whether he'd like to sit for a spell and share a glass of lemonade. Like his father, Falwell won over people with his wit and raconteurship. He was a genuinely likeable, if overly chatty, kid.

Local pastors didn't find Falwell so likeable, though, especially after they found he was canvassing for congregants in their "territory." Falwell would craftily suggest that folks attend the night service at his church, so as not to appear he was pilfering. But the idea of the evening service was to get visitors enthused enough to then come to morning services and join Thomas Road. The local pastors were wise to the young upstart. They told him to back off, not realizing they were trying to scare someone who had just faced down the entire 2,000-member Baptist Bible Fellowship.

Falwell did not back down. Instead, he and his volunteers jotted down the results of every encounter on a yellow legal pad: names, addresses, occupations, history of church affilliation. It was as if he were compiling a census, and was a businesslike approach most country churches never bothered with. Like a salesman generating hot leads, Falwell devised what he called his "triple whammy." Each home would get a personal visit, a follow-up phone call from a volunteer, and a newsletter.[17] Disguised as church news, the newsletter was really a recruiting pitch. Writing longhand on a sheet of paper, he welcomed new members and touted the growth of his embryonic church. A volunteer typed up the notes and created headlines using press-on letters, then reproduced the page on a borrowed mimeograph machine. Within a year he and his volunteers had canvassed nearly every home in Lynchburg, some as many as five times. He called it "saturation evangelism."

It was also a bit of smart sociology. He knew that most people join churches based on a human factor, such as a friend who suggests they attend a sermon, or a pastor who makes a personal connection. To most new members of his church, Falwell became a trusted confidante. He gave everyone his home telephone number and made himself available day or night, just as his father had in his last days. He began conducting wedding services and funerals for church members. He made hospital visits three days a week to pray with congregation members or members of their families. He counseled couples whose marriages had hit the rocks and parents of kids who drank too much.

The trust parishoners gave to Falwell extended to their financial affairs. A lot of folks knew Falwell's entrepreneurial father and assumed that the son knew something about business, too. For some families he became their unofficial financial adviser, turning their spending patterns into profit-and-loss statements. His working-class congregation had little disposable wealth; he would have to push them hard.

"Put God in your budget," he commanded, telling them to place "tithing" at the top of their list of monthly expenses. Those who were slow adopting such spiritual math got a scolding. One Sunday morning at Thomas Road Baptist Church (TRBC) he laid it on thick:

> Satan knows how to tempt you. The time comes around to pay your tithes and offerings. Financially, you're behind on your payments and you don't know how in the world you're going to buy the groceries or meet the car payment. It's school time, or time to buy a license. You face all kinds of excuses, bills and problems. You have God's money, God's tithe, and Satan tells you: "Why don't you hold it back for a week or two. After all, you need that car to get to church. After all, the children are a responsibility. You'll be able to pay your tithe back later." And soon, you begin stealing from the Lord.[18]

Where some saw guile behind his aggressiveness, others admired his zealotry. Whichever it was, it worked. Thomas Road Baptist Church, started with rejects from his own hometown church, now had *triple* the membership of the Park Avenue church. He knew God was driving this growth and believed it was a sign that he was destined to expand his congregation far beyond its small-town roots. He would do it the same way Charles Fuller had invaded his own home on those early Sunday mornings—over the air.

And why not? Religious revivalism was radio's fastest-growing genre. Billy Graham started his *Hour of Decision* in 1950. Rex Humbard went live with his sermons in 1953. Oral Roberts brought his preaching to the air in 1954. One of Falwell's favorite hometown radio stations was WBRG, whose AM country-and-western format he'd listen to on drives with Macel. Falwell went to see the station's owner in the summer of 1956. The owner just happened to be hunting for religious content and was delighted to broadcast Falwell's daily sermons, offering to do it at a rate of seven dollars for thirty minutes. Falwell was soon broadcasting each weekday morning at 6:30 A.M., opening his program with a prerecorded blaze of trumpets and choir music. The signal was only 1,000 watts, but that was strong enough to reach homes forty miles away.

Falwell modeled his entire broadcast around Fuller's *Old Fashioned Revival Hour,* calling it the *Old Time Gospel Hour.* He played records by George Beverly Shea, one of Billy Graham's singers, and brought vocalists from Thomas Road to sing. Letters began to arrive from farther and farther away—he read them all on the air. He announced neighborhoods he'd visit soon and performed a roll call of those who had been saved. At that time in the morning, the show could be heard in Lynchburg's barbershops and beauty salons. People listened intently to his list of those saved. In a small town like Lynchburg, names would be instantly recognized and curiosity would be piqued as to why a friend, a neighbor, or a relative had joined Falwell's new church.

The growing crowd attending Sunday morning services was causing a serious space problem at the Donald Duck building. In early 1957, Falwell called S. Frank Pratt, owner of the Lynchburg Oil Company, to ask for a $5,000 unsecured loan to build an addition to his church. Pratt had been a good friend of Carey's; he agreed to the loan. Over the next few years, Falwell would construct an annex to the church, then build an entirely new church in the shape of an octagon, inspired by the eight-sided rooms laid out in plans for Thomas Jefferson's summer home in Poplar Forest. The building conveyed an air of stately antebellum elegance, just the image Falwell was striving for.

Falwell's radio show was working financial magic: piles of checks arrived daily. But he spent the money as fast as he got it. He had taken yet another page from Fuller, using his risky formula for growth. Fuller bought broadcast time with borrowed funds, paying them back when contributions arrived from new listeners. That put Fuller in a chronic cycle of debt. When Fuller paid for airtime to beam his message to a new market, it typically took two months for contributions from the new audience to cover the purchase of airtime. The danger, of course, was that not every new market could be counted on to cover the costs to reach it.

The costs of radio evangelizing was small change compared to the money he would spend to take the next step. Television, a brand new medium, was transforming the way people practiced their faith and thought about God. A handful of superstars had already staked claims on the small screen. Falwell had no time to lose.

3. Microphone Missionary

A T the dawn of the Baby Boom, no one delivered religious drama quite like Roman Catholic Archbishop Fulton J. Sheen. He spoke with the jaunty elegance of a Hollywood star, and looked like one. Sheen wore a black cassock lined with purple piping, a red cape that draped to the floor, a gleaming gold crucifix, and a small skull cap. He performed before a live audience at the Adelphi Theatre in midtown Manhattan, though no one thought he'd gain much attention. He appeared in a time slot known as an "obituary," meaning the producer believed he had no chance against his 8 P.M. competitor. Sheen was up against another newcomer to television, Milton Berle, host of *Texaco Star Theater*.

Sheen's show, *Life Is Worth Living*, often laced with anti-Communist themes, appealed to an audience beyond Christians. One of his most caustic performances was a dramatic recital of the burial scene in Shakespeare's *Julius Caesar*. He substituted the names of Stalinist leaders in place of Caesar, Cassius, Mark Antony, and Brutus, ending the broadcast by thundering, "Stalin must one day meet his judgment!" A week later the Soviet leader died of a stroke.

Sheen's ratings ascended toward Heaven during his first season, stealing viewers from Berle. Uncle Miltie marveled at the success of his Catholic rival, quipping, "And he did it using old material." Sheen received an Emmy Award in 1952 as the year's "most outstanding television personality," trumping competitors Edward R. Murrow and Lucille Ball. In his remarks to the academy, Sheen said, "I'd like to thank my writers: Matthew, Mark, Luke, and John."

Sheen differed from most pioneers of religious television in that he did not seek contributions. He had a sponsor—not the Catholic church, but the Admiral Corporation. It was a luxury Rex Humbard, then building a television empire at his Calvary Temple in Akron, Ohio, would have loved. Humbard's infectious enthusiasm, braced by a smooth Arkansas drawl, made his leap from radio to television seamless. Tithing from his television viewers would help him underwrite a four-million-dollar, 5,000-seat "Cathedral of Tomorrow," the first church ever constructed for a television audience. It moved on a hydraulic stage lit by thousands of red, white, and blue light bulbs on a giant cross.

Falwell was fascinated by the theatrics of these new televangelists, but what truly astounded him was the secular media's embrace of Billy Graham. Graham was an obscure country preacher until 1949, the year he brought his tent revival meetings to Los Angeles and attracted the notice of William Randolph Hearst. Graham's fierce anti-Communist rhetoric dazzled Hearst, who became an instant fan. Thus, came a telegram one day from Hearst to his editors with a classic directive: "Puff Graham."[1] Hearst-owned newspapers, magazines, and movies did just that, and Graham's career took off. Five years later Graham found himself on the cover of *Time*.

With this formidable competition, Falwell planned his own launch on television just a few months after the debut of his radio broadcasts in 1956. But how would he be different? He began by appearing each Sunday evening for thirty minutes on WLVA Channel 13, bringing the *Gospel Hour* to television. It cost him ninety dollars per broadcast. His voice on those first shows had a tinny resonance. He spoke rapidly, with a nasal twang. Sitting at a small wooden table with no props, Falwell offered his thoughts with a composed eloquence that translated well to the grainy, black-and-white television screen. He did not predict Armageddon, handle snakes, speak in tongues, or smack people in the forehead, pronouncing them "Saved!" He did not take off his jacket, throw air punches, or work up a rainstorm of sweat on his brow.

Instead, he related stories from the one hundred homes he'd visit each day; it was all the material he needed. He told inspiring yarns about what God did for people, recounting hair-raising tales of drug abuse and alcoholism. He related tragic childhoods, how people lived lives of crime, survived suicide attempts, and tried to commit murder before turning to God. Falwell had grown up on the wrong side of the tracks; he could relate to it all. Just a few years earlier he had headed up a street gang; his father was a pistol-packing bootlegger who killed his own brother. His uncle beat up newspaper reporters.

More helpful to Falwell's career, probably, was his father's gift of gab. Carey's raconteurship and pugnacious self-confidence had rubbed off on his son. Even at his young age, he was a master storyteller. His renditions of people's dark misfortunes and spectacular redemption was a kind of religious reality TV.

As much as Falwell admired the new televangelists, he was disgusted by their one-size-fits-all, ecumenical theology. They were watering down the faith, he thought. In 1957, Billy Graham's soaring career caused a falling out with his longtime mentor, John R. Rice, the Citizen Kane of fundamentalist publishing. Rice had soured on Graham, essentially accusing him of theological backsliding by working with liberal evangelicals to produce his giant rallies. Graham would also have a falling out with Bob Jones, the namesake of the fundamentalist university he attended, who called Graham an "apostate." Falwell sensed an opening created by Graham's perceived drift from fundamentalist orthodoxy. He imagined himself the guardian, perhaps even the new face of fundamentalism.

Looking directly into the camera, fingers locked, the young, earnest preacher transferred the in-person intimacy he had with members of his church to his electronic audience. This intimacy was repaid first by curiosity, then loyalty. As new stations were added to carry his broadcast, new faces showed up at his Sunday services. A couple from Roanoke, a group of retirees from Charlottesville, a family of seven from Appomattox. They all heard or watched the *Gospel Hour* and drove to Lynchburg to see Falwell in person.

When they came to church, they were expected to tithe 10 percent of their income. As Falwell reminded them, "If a Christian is not giving money to God, he is not obedient." In fact, he said, that 10 percent already belonged to God. Only when a church member gave beyond that 10 percent—an offering known as sacrificial giving—would their gift really be significant. Falwell began to come up with other ways for his booming membership to contribute. One weekend he tore out one hundred pages of names from the Lynchburg phone book and handed one to each of the same number of volunteers who had come forward at a Sunday sermon. Then he handed each person a script:

> Hello, I'm Mrs. Jones from the Thomas Road Baptist Church. My pastor, Jerry Falwell, asked me to phone you to ask you to come to our services tomorrow. Dr. Falwell will be speaking on the subject, "Where Are the Dead?" He felt you might have some interest in this message and wants you to be his personal guest for his class in the morning.[2]

As Falwell grew his ministry, the phone calls and letters from his audience delivered some stinging feedback. He was suddenly aware of being judged. Most letters came steeped with praise (and cash). But a few pushed his buttons, especially the ones from viewers who watched the *Gospel Hour* and questioned his credentials for advancing his vision of an infallible, inerrant Bible. *Young man, we are no longer a nation of Puritans. Find some proper schoolin' before you preach on the Good Book.* Even oblique messages would set him off. For all the gravitas his pulpit bestowed, Falwell sensed that to many, especially city dwellers, he was an unlettered outcast from the hills who used God as a cloak of respectability.

Before he was saved, he never spent much time pondering existential issues; he spent even less time doing so after he found Christ. In the midst of a financial crisis, he would pray. In the midst of a health crisis, he would pray. Where the Bible seemed less-than-authoritative, he would pray for clarity. When his prayers weren't answered he would pray more and meditate on how much additional prayer he should practice. These habits of mind focused his energies and often gave him answers, but they also left with him with little capacity for self-reflection. When he received constructive criticism or faced honest philosophical disagreement he confused it with personal animus. Perhaps subconsciously, he identified with the qualities he ascribed to the Bible itself: inerrant to a fault. "Don't pay attention to all the criticism, Jerry," said Macel. "They are really just attacks on the Lord."

When he thought of criticism in those terms, Falwell's brain processed antipathy differently. An attack became raw fuel. It made him work longer, harder, faster, and smarter. *Jealous, petty critics will never cause me to doubt myself. I will not stray from doctrine,* he thought. He would mentally quarantine criticism. Over time, Falwell would harness the energy of his critics and use it to his own advantage. "Either my dad was the greatest actor alive, or he had the thickest skin of anyone I've ever known," says son Jonathan.

One criticism that was certainly grounded in truth: Falwell was not good with money. Macel, then working as a teller at First National Bank, kept the books for his growing ministry. "She never even let Dad have his own checking account," said Jerry Jr. Macel was concerned that Falwell's radio and television broadcasts simply cost too much money. Contributions were being used to buy blocks of airtime, with little left for anything else. It was an expensive means of growth. Was there a cheaper way? Falwell put the question to some of the businessmen who were early members of Thomas Road. Listening to the advice of haberdashers and department-store owners led him to a simple conclusion: the greatest business innovation of his generation was the shopping center.

Lynchburg's anchor stores, like Sears and JCPenney created enough foot traffic to support smaller businesses around them, which in turn fed traffic back to the anchor stores, and one another. One businessman suggested Falwell think of his church in such retail terms. The notion intrigued him. He envisioned ministries around his mother church like spokes in a wheel. At the center would be income from tithing, a steady 10 percent from each church member. At the periphery would be larger gifts in the form of sacrificial giving, underwriting the ministries themselves and bringing growth to the church. But what would these ministries be?

Booze had killed Falwell's father; drinking was a serious problem among some members of Thomas Road. Why not start a ministry for alcoholics? It would give Falwell cathartic satisfaction in saving others from the fate suffered by Carey. A home for alcoholics might even bring some good publicity to his spiritual ventures. He had no money to start such a ministry, but discussed the idea with his older brother Lewis, whose 165-acre farm in Appomattox County would be its first home (it would later move to another, smaller farm in Amherst County). Falwell conceived of it as a kind of Christian kibbutz. While residents were drying out they would grow their own food and perform chores communally. It would be a monument to their father, argued Falwell to Lewis. When it opened, conditions were primitive: there was no heat, running water, or electricity. The church didn't yet own the Amherst County farm, said Falwell in a 1959 story in *The News,* "but hopes God will provide the money for its purchase."[3]

The church had begun as a congregation of blue-collar retirees and older women. Now Thomas Road was attracting parents who needed to park their kids somewhere during service. Falwell had the answer: a Sunday-school ministry. Among the school's volunteer teaching force was Bill Newton, a former Oregon highway patrolman whose class for nine-year-old boys was called The Tree House Club. A log fence stood at the entrance next to a tall cardboard tree. Newton employed a yo-yo champion and a barefoot hillbilly preacher to draw kids in. A "nutty professor" recounted Bible stories, notably those that knocked down ideas about evolution. A quiz was later held wherein correct answers were rewarded by the student attaching a plastic limb to a four-foot dummy of Satan hanging from a ceiling. When all the limbs were attached, Satan was indeed hanged, and the kids cheered.[4]

For older kids, Falwell created another Sunday program, "junior church." He remembered that his father's passenger bus-business had flourished not just because of the routes chosen, but the friendly drivers who turned riders into friends. Falwell leased a fleet of fifteen school buses to pick up children all over town and handpicked the drivers. He chose colorful, disarming characters and asked them to trace their Sunday school pickup routes the day before they would drive them. On Saturday the drivers would walk along streets, pockets filled with bubblegum, knocking door to door and asking whether parents would like to have their kids picked up by the church bus and taken to Sunday school for free. After church the kids raced back to the parking lots, where hamburgers and Kool-Aid awaited them. A family whose kid attended Sunday school at Thomas Road frequently became church members themselves.

Falwell himself would soon become a parent. His first son, Jerry Jr., was born on Father's Day in 1962. If he built a home for alcoholics in memory of his father, why shouldn't he start an elementary school for his kids? A school run by the church would also be a most convenient way for him to sidestep the desegregation of public schools ordered by the U.S. Supreme Court's *Brown v. Board of Education* decision, which Falwell feared. In 1967, the church began the first classes for his Liberty Christian Academy, offering grades kindergarten to six. Within five years, it would be a K-12 school with six hundred students. All three of Falwell's children, Jerry Jr., Jonathan, and Jeannie, would attend.

In the early years these new school ventures were paid for, in part, by two traveling salesmen: Jerry Falwell and his eight-year-old son, Jerry Jr. They took trips during the week to sell books produced by his printing ministry and tapes of musical performances of his church singers. They would travel in Falwell's Buick Wildcat, the trunk jammed with audio tapes and gospel tracts, and show up at churches and fund-raising events at towns where his *Gospel Hour* was heard on the air. Sales were so brisk, recalls Jerry Jr., that on some days he found himself stuffing cash into his socks.

The product they were selling was based on an unalloyed vision: an uncompromising, orthodox Christian doctrine. It was precisely the opposite of what mainline Protestant churches offered in the 1960s. Membership in liberal denominations had taken a nosedive. Falwell believed this was because these churches reflected the culture, rather than led it. "In the 1960s, couples were being married in balloons or in carriages; readings in church included passages from Timothy Leary and Kahlil Gibran; at one wedding in New York the bride wore a G-string; at a Northeastern seminary the students prepared for the Eucharist by smoking marijuana; a Baptist clergyman came on national TV to play the guitar with his toes."[5]

Falwell ridiculed such laxity, terming it undignified and ungodly. Perhaps it was. But this did not stop him from giving his own services a touch of P. T. Barnum. He turned over his pulpit to a Christian karate expert who gave testimony to God's power by breaking a 2,000-pound block of ice with his hand. He introduced his congregation to a wrestler from the midwest who, at seven feet, eight inches, was believed to the world's tallest Christian.[6] He once assembled fifteen of the church's deacons on a table, along with his seven-year-old son, Jerry Jr., and watched Paul Anderson, then the world's strongest man, lift all sixteen.

These stunts always drew a crowd, but when visitors came to Thomas Road the main event was Falwell himself—and his preoccupation of the moment. A recurring theme was the battle with "the enemy," Falwell's term for Satan:

> The moment you entered the family of God, Satan declared war on you. Satan is a roaring lion who goes about devouring those whom he can. The born-again believer is his prime target. Satan never relaxes. He never pillows his head. When you get up in the morning, the enemy already is there waiting for you. When you go to your job, the adversary beats you there. At night when you lay your head down on the pillow, the tempter is standing, waiting, watching. Satan is looking for every opportunity to knock you out of fellowship with God.[7]

Falwell would recite every alias Satan was known by. "Some call him the Devil. Others call him Beelzebub, Belial, the Obstructor, the Tempter, the Evil One, the Accuser, the Prince of Demons, the ruler of this World, the Prince of the Power of the Air. Whatever you call him, he is the Enemy and he is real!"[8]

His sermons were gaining focus, but Falwell's political intelligence was still unrefined. He seemed oblivious to the coming fact of desegregation. It had been a decade since the *Brown v. Board of Education* decision. Southern states were now in varying stages of carrying out its mandate that public schools be integrated. The South, a culture which was born, bred, and raised on a system of separating the races, was now being told to abandon it. Falwell seemed to be in denial. His rival, Billy Graham, refused to speak before segregated audiences and had paid Martin Luther King's bail to spring him from jail. Graham declared that there was no scriptural basis for segregation. Falwell believed there was, citing Noah's curse on Ham, in Genesis.

Falwell condemned his fellow Baptist ministers, making veiled assertions that some were in bed with Communists. He said pastors and ministers who challenged segregation had no business engaging the larger culture, much less national politics. Those who do were engaging in a "civil wrongs" movement. In March 1965, Falwell made his oft-quoted speech, "Ministers and Marches," condemning the involvement of Christian ministers in politics. The growing counterculture was scaring the wits out of Falwell. "Ministers and Marches" was his angry rejoinder. Falwell would later try to make this speech disappear. He would also regret taking so long to support some of the moral crusades launched in the 1960s by his fellow ministers. As Falwell told writer Dinesh D'Souza in 1983, "It took me several years to get segregation flushed out of my soul."

Falwell took heart in the fact that his Sunday school, church, and Christian academy were growing like gangbusters. His ministries weren't making money, but he didn't care: he wanted growth for growth's sake. He now began thinking about the next logical spoke in the wheel of his church: a university. He would thwart the counterculture with a culture of his own, insulated by its location and its doctrine. He envisioned his campus as a Harvard for Christian intellectuals, a Notre Dame for athletics, and a Brigham Young University for fundamentalists. It was a bold vision for a man who never attended a university. Luring college-age kids to Lynchburg would be a radical flip in the demographic target of his own church, whose early members had been mostly over fifty.

The genius behind his idea for Lynchburg Baptist College (later called Liberty Baptist College), in sales terms, is that it would be the ultimate feeder ministry for his anchor store, the church. A university would bring a permanent constituency. Students, faculty members, and university workers would all become church members. "Lynchburg Baptist College will be the secret ingredient that will make the Thomas Road Baptist Church the largest gathered congregation since Pentecost," promised Falwell.[9]

Falwell thrived on grandiose dreams and enjoyed the company of those with whom he could share them. He also enjoyed a good old-fashioned intellectual smackdown. He was not afraid to bring people into his inner circle who had brains and use them to challenge their boss. One was Elmer Towns, a wisecracking, imperious former Christian college president who met Falwell on a visit to Falwell's Sunday school in 1968. Falwell called Towns one night and the two sketched out the makings of the university in a one-hour and fifteen-minute phone call between Towns in Wheaton, Illinois, and Falwell in Lynchburg.

"I said three things to Jerry," recalls Towns. "The university ought to be like Wheaton College, without the compromisin' over things like coed dorms; it oughta be like Bob Jones University, without their rigid rules; and it oughta be like Baptist Bible College without the hillbilly influence."

Falwell didn't mind being told how to build his own university; he would hire Towns to help do it. Falwell promoted the new school on his *Gospel Hour* broadcasts, promising a preeminent education with Christian values at its core and easy-to-obtain scholarships. He referred to it as the "University of God." Towns put out the word to dozens of pastors and educators that Falwell's college had begun enrollment. By late spring, both were shocked by the result. A total of eight students had enrolled.

A red-faced Towns met Falwell in his office in early June. "Jerry, this is not good. You're going to be embarrassed because you're starting what looks like a two-bit school. I'm going to be embarrassed because all my academic friends warned me not to come out here to Appalachia."

Falwell leaned back in his chair. "We need some serious marketing," he said dryly. "Let's put an ad in every Christian publication we know."

Towns knew the idea was folly. "Jerry, it's June 1. By the time these ads appear, it'll be September 1. School starts on September 8."

Falwell nodded. He thought a moment, then his face lit up. "Here's what we do. Offer a free trip to Israel to every pastor who enrolls five students."

Towns was dumbfounded. Was Falwell suggesting they start their university by holding a sweepstakes? Well, yes. Towns thought hard for a moment, then offered a revision. "Forget the pastors. Let's offer a free trip to every student who enrolls and promises to stay at Lynchburg Baptist College for the first year."

"Give the trip to the students?" Falwell paused, then slammed his open hand on his desk. "Let's do it. We'll figure out how to pay for it later," he chuckled.

Falwell trumpeted the trip on the *Gospel Hour*, at Sunday sermons, in radio interviews, and at every public appearance he made. He sent a direct mailing to his entire congregation, promising that every student who stayed at the school for the first year would get a free trip to Israel. "Imagine walking where Jesus walked. Study in the Promised Land!" said Falwell in his promos. By August, Falwell and Towns had 154 applications. Of those, ninety stayed on to complete the first semester.

In January 1972, the entire student body boarded the cruise ship *Orpheus* bound for Israel. Along for the trip was another two hundred lay people who had signed up for the voyage. At the Bay of Haifa, Falwell assembled the crowd for a special announcement. Looking toward the Shrine of the Báb and its terraces on Mount Carmel, Falwell began: "Welcome to a magical place. It cost us fifty-five thousand dollars to bring our kids here. They are young people starting something that will become the greatest Christian university in the world. They are champions for Christ on their maiden voyage. Is there anyone here who can help us pay the cost of rewarding these young men and women for their courage to take this trip with us? Please raise your hand." Surrounded by Jerry's kids, almost every hand among the two hundred went up. Salad bowls appeared from nowhere, floating from person to person. They were soon piled high with cash and pledges totaling $93,000.

It was money desperately needed. Tuition to the unaccredited college brought in a mere $150 per student. Attending Lynchburg Baptist College in its first few years was akin to competing in an episode of *Survivor*. Classes were held in stairways and hallways. There was no space at the church for dorms so Falwell sent his students to live in shacks on an island in the middle of the James River—low-lying land that was frequently underwater. Falwell put more students in an abandoned hospital and rooms at old downtown hotels with "no television, no telephone, no air-conditioning," recalls LBC graduate Mark Lowry. "Our beds were those metal jobs they'd purchased from an insane asylum."[10]

Falwell knew he would need to create a residential campus of some kind, but had no idea where he'd get the land or how he'd pay for it. The absence of any classrooms—much less a larger university campus—did not deter him from advertising that he had both. An early catalog carried a photo of a "Division of Business." It was actually a shot of the United Virginal Bank in Lynchburg. On a page describing the school of religion, Falwell ran a photo of a Civil War–era brick chapel shaded by trees. The photo was not of a building belonging to his school, but of Lee Chapel, the burial site of General Lee, fifty miles away.[11]

The school's most pressing problem wasn't classrooms, but student housing. In a meeting with his church deacons, one suggested a bond offering to ease the housing crunch. Liberty would soon float $6.5 million in construction bonds to buy land and build student dorms. The bonds were purchased by 1,632 investors in twenty-five states over the next two years.

With some of this cash in hand, Falwell asked William Burruss Jr., a Lynchburg land developer who had joined the church, what he knew about available land nearby to start a campus. Burruss had a friend at U.S. Gypsum, which owned 2,100 acres of nearby Candler's Mountain. The timing of Falwell's inquiry was perfect: U.S.

Gypsum, then in the midst of battling asbestos claims, had begun divesting its assets. The company offered its 2,100 acres to Falwell for $1,250,000. In the coming decade Falwell would buy up another nine parcels of pine-studded land adjoining the U.S. Gypsum property, annexing nearly 5,000 acres.

Falwell's radio and television ministries, along with church volunteers who volunteered to launch door-to-door recruitment campaigns in Campbell, Bedford, and Amherst counties, kept his congregation growing at a rapid clip. The flood of cash gave him money to buy printing presses for TRBC that churned out leaflets, bulletins, newspapers, booklets, and Bible-study courses, all of which drew new members and solicited donations. Church membership was approaching 7,000. His gross income was one million dollars and the church went on a hiring binge, bringing his staff to eighty assistant pastors, teachers, and administrators.

In the first decade of his ministry, Falwell had traveled mostly by car. That was fine when most of his church growth came from his hometown's metropolitan region. Now he was chasing dollars in competition with other ministries on a statewide, and increasingly nationwide basis. There were thirty-eight syndicated religious programs on the air in 1970; by 1975, the number had reached sixty-five. Over those same years, the combined audience for television evangelists went from 9.8 million to 20.8 million viewers.[12] To compete, Falwell would have to take his appearances, rallies and recitals far outside Virginia. In the spring of 1971, he bought an eight-seat Cessna 414 for $225,000. The next year he traded up, spending $600,000 on a roomier Convair 580, which seated thirty-two. This bigger craft meant he could travel to any city where the *Gospel Hour* was broadcast without refueling.

The 1970s looked like they would be a miracle decade for Falwell until he woke up on the morning of January 23, 1973. That day's edition of the *Lynchburg News* carried a story about a U.S. Supreme Court decision that ruled unconstitutional all state laws banning voluntary abortions before the third month. Falwell was so obsessed with the growth of his church and university that he had been blindsided by *Roe v. Wade*. He was stunned and, for the first time, had no idea what to do. All of his energies, his fund-raising, his travel schedule were locked up for months. Even if he freed up time to fight the decision, what would that actually accomplish?

A few months later Falwell got a call from an investigator at the Securities and Exchange Commission in Washington. The SEC believed the bonds Falwell sold may not have been backed by sufficient assets for collateral. The agency would soon file a federal complaint against Falwell's church, accusing the organization of "fraud and deceit." The SEC suspected that the church was about $9 million in debt beyond what was owed to bondholders. It was impossible to establish exactly what had been spent by Falwell or even where most of the proceeds from the bonds were. Falwell had taken over the bookkeeping from Macel and he practiced none of his father Carey's accounting discipline. The church ledgers were a mess. The only oversight of his spending was the church treasurer—a part-time volunteer.

In fact, much of the money had been spent to add stations nationwide to the *Gospel Hour* network. A few days before a federal judge was to hear the case in August 1973, Falwell asked his congregation for their prayers. "The devil is after us," he intoned. "God knows we've done nothing wrong." Falwell explained the situation in Biblical terms to his church members, in this case, David versus Goliath. He persuaded his congregation, as he often would, that they were all players on the Bible's dispensationalist stage.

A more secular explanation was that Falwell was a sloppy accountant and apparently ignorant of disclosures he was required to make for the bonds. He was cleared of "intentional wrongdoing," but he was hardly off the hook. The judge's ruling had the effect of calling the bonds. Suddenly liable for $6.5 million he didn't have, Falwell was required to hand oversight of the church's financial affairs to a group of five local businesspeople appointed by the judge until the debt was repaid.

The SEC action was the first outside financial reality check Falwell had ever received. It shook him to his core. He was shocked that the federal government could suddenly swoop in and turn his world upside-down. He blamed the stewardship department of the church for making misstatements on the bond prospectus, which the SEC said was evidence that Falwell had engaged in deceit.[13] The prospectus noted that Falwell's Christian children's academy was accredited (it wasn't) and had exaggerated the value of church assets (based on a donor's written intention to offer a gift, without having the gift in hand).[14] The crisis brought Falwell's university expansion plans to a halt.

It would take Falwell three years to pay off the $6.5 million. Meeting monthly with his "advisory committee," he was convinced to hire an accountant and public-relations firm. The group demonstrated how crucial an independent board can be. They realized that Falwell was sitting on an untapped goldmine—his own faithful donors. They hired Jerry Huntsinger, a copywriting genius and one of the rising stars in nonprofit fund-raising. He suggested Falwell deepen his relationship with potential donors by creating affinity clubs grouped around different aspects of his ministries. It would be a bit like attaching a solid rim to the spokes of his church. Devotional associations with names like the Pastor's Team, Doorkeepers, Station Sponsors, and the Ten Thousand Club would be created. They gave people a strong sense of ownership without having to make a large contribution. The best performing group turned out to be Faith Partners, formed to support Falwell's television ministry.

"The empire was built on Faith Partners," says Towns, who traveled with Falwell on his Cessna to dozens of churches and fund-raising events in the 1970s. "Doug Oldham would meet us at a church and sing, Jerry would preach, and I would talk about the college. At the end of the sermon, Jerry would ask: 'How many of you will become a Faith Partner and promise to give us ten dollars per month?' Falwell would pass out a packet of a dozen envelopes stamped with prepaid postage. In a congregation of, say, four hundred people, maybe fifty people would agree, translating to an instant five hundred dollars in new income a month. Like a telethon host, Falwell would return to the stage, saying, "I'm going to press you. If another twenty-five people stand up, I'll ask Doug Oldham to sing his favorite song, 'The King Is Coming Again.'"

Every Sunday morning, his ten-dollars-per-month contributors would be plugged with an on-screen credit during the *Gospel Hour,* just as Bishop Sheen had plugged the Admiral Corporation on his own show. Says Towns, "Jerry always had the ability to make it personal." Eventually, 110,000 Faith Partners would send ten dollars per month (for a total annual take of $13 million).

Falwell used some of this money to help eliminate the bond debt, but he soon figured out a novel way to help pay the balance off: raising money from students themselves. In late 1974, Falwell challenged that year's class to give an extra one hundred dollars apiece beyond their normal tithing at church after the Christmas break. They answered the call: cars, clothes, radios, furniture, and musical instruments were sold off, generating $200,000. Then Falwell organized a fund-raising tour across the United States with members of the school's chorale group, who gave up eleven months of their education (but received college credit) for the tour. Traveling day and night, they performed at army bases, shopping malls, banquets, and church services. They sang their hearts out, followed by a sermon from Falwell and a request for offerings. Falwell would fly home Wednesdays and Sundays for services at TRBC. In less than a year they appeared in three hundred churches in thirty-six states, logging 80,000 miles.[15]

The mission sometimes required travel to hostile territory. One such visit took them to Seattle, a citadel of the counterculture, in March of 1975. Falwell and his students gathered in a small, musty gymnasium at the Seattle Center, a complex built for the 1962 World's Fair, anchored by the 605-foot Space Needle nearby. Just a few years earlier the city had hosted the Trips Festival, a daylong blast of searing acid rock bathed in light shows and pot smoke, where a "psychedelicatessen" offered green Jell-O and bananas with chocolate sauce.[16]

Some 250 fundamentalist youth, churchgoers, and their guests arrived and sat themselves down on rows of folding chairs in the gym. The LBC singers lit into a string of standards. Church members clapped and threw their hands in the air. The power of the gospel was filling the room until about halfway through the recital, when a massive vibration shook the gym. The singers stopped. Had a bus had hit the building? No, it was more like a sound wave. Then it came again; the sound was unmistakable. It was the earsplitting chords of an electric guitar.[17] Falwell had booked his Christian sing-along just down the hall from the Seattle Center, where 14,000 fans had gathered for a Led Zeppelin concert.

Falwell flapped his arms, motioning the singers to start again from the top. It wasn't easy belting "How Great Thou Art!" over "Whole Lotta Love." At the end of the service Falwell shook hands and ministered to those ready to receive Christ, trying to ignore Robert Plant's wailing over 50,000-watt Marshall amplifiers. He clasped a hand on the shoulder of each person that approached him, yelling at them to take up Bible study and to devote themselves to their local church. When the room cleared Falwell motioned to a group of five Liberty students to come with him on an assignment. He wanted to see firsthand the source of this electronic assault.

In his three-piece suit and a troupe of cleanly coiffed followers from Virginia, Falwell cut a slightly incongruous figure as he entered the arena. The lobby was filled with shaggy-haired kids in jeans and sandals. Thick clouds of reefer smoke hovered overhead. Falwell was astounded to see the array of delivery devices used to get high: kids were using pipes, bongs, super stones, and plain old joints rolled in Zig-Zag papers. Glassy-eyed youth stumbled down aisles. Seattle police were taking away a few who could no longer stand. Couples were fondling each other in their seats as Robert Plant twirled onstage like a dervish.

For Falwell, a man who did not smoke, drink, swear, or dance, it must have been a Dante-like spectacle. Falwell was more concerned about his students. "It was quite an experience for our kids, who are used to the preaching of the gospel, the joyfulness and radiance of Christian life, for them to walk from that into what was really a coliseum of death," he said.[18]

Falwell returned to Lynchburg to face one more colossal disappointment: the election of Jimmy Carter. Carter was a fellow Baptist, but in Falwell's view he was also part of the backsliding, tolerant liberal church contributing to the culture's moral drift. His famous interview in *Playboy* in 1976, in which he admitted having lust in his heart for women other than his wife, so enraged Falwell that he held a press conference to denounce it. Part of Falwell's ire toward Carter came from his knowledge that Carter had won the 1976 election with help from evangelicals, in spite of the fact that in the closing weeks of the election it became clear Carter's theology was anything but conservative. He was pro-choice, supported the ERA, and liked to have a beer once in a while. Falwell considered Carter an illegitimate Baptist.

To pay off the final balance of what he owed on Liberty's bonds, Falwell launched a successor to his debt relief tour with an "I Love America" campaign, traveling to forty-four state capitals with an even bigger group of chorale singers. State officials and members of Congress flocked to these performances, as did the press. In one rally in Little Rock, Arkansas, Gov. Bill Clinton joined Falwell on the steps of the Capitol. The rallies drew so much press attention that in October 1978, *Esquire* would name Falwell "the next Billy Graham." By the end of that year, Falwell had raised $20 million.

In the summer of 1979, Falwell called Towns at his office on campus and asked Towns to accompany him on a trip to Murfreesboro,

Tennessee. They were to see Towns's old friend, John R. Rice, the legendary fundamentalist publisher of *Sword of the Lord.* Falwell had met Rice many times and spoke at Sword of the Lord conferences, but now Falwell had a pressing favor to ask of Rice.

Born in 1895, Rice was the ultimate rock-ribbed fundamentalist. He once rode his horse 120 miles to attend a Baptist seminary. But he did not believe in churches that tithe and thought fundamentalists had no business engaging secular culture on matters of God. Over lunch, Falwell did not mention the talks he had been having with Richard Viguerie and others about forming a national political organization to defeat liberal members of Congress and to elect a conservative president steeped in Christian values. Falwell only discussed expanding his Baptist college and the greater need for world evangelization.

"John, we want to double Liberty's size in the next five years," said Falwell, fingers locked together as if he were delivering a television sermon. "We are going to make it a Notre Dame for fundamentalists. We could surely use your help. We're wondering whether you'd consider letting us add the names of your folks to our mailing list so we can reach every young person in America and bring them to Liberty."

What Falwell was after was Rice's coveted *Sword of the Lord* mailing list. It contained the names of 200,000 pastors in every church in the Southern Baptist Convention. The holy men on Rice's list were "influencers," capable of mobilizing their flock to write letters, make phone calls to wealthy parishioners, and write checks. "Of course we can help," said the eighty-four-year-old Rice. "Do you want the names today?" Falwell nodded, then flashed Towns a Cheshire-cat grin. "It was a huge coup," says Towns.

Later that afternoon Towns and Falwell jumped in a taxi and headed to Rice's local bank. They walked inside and were met by a manager who took them to a vault. Inside were copies of Rice's massive directory, saved on giant spools of tapes resembling movie reels from the 1940s. Falwell and Towns lugged the containers back to the airport. On the return flight they felt as if they had just raided Fort Knox. The analogy isn't far off. Lists like this would be the building blocks in assembling a two-million-name mailing list of followers. Falwell would use the resources of his ministries to build the Moral Majority, and use the Moral Majority to raise the visibility of his university. Liberty would eventually become a whistlestop on presidential campaigns for Republican candidates. Speaking at Falwell's university would become a symbolic right of passage for any candidate courting the Religious Right.

After the presidential race of 1980, some media outlets would personally credit Falwell with delivering the voting margin that produced Ronald Reagan's victory. Falwell would, in fact, receive far more help from Reagan than the Religious Right could ever deliver to Republicans. At the end of Reagan's first term, income to Falwell's church doubled, soaring to over $100 million. Lynchburg became the fifth largest direct-mail center in the country. As powerful a fund-raising tool Reagan was to Falwell, it would not be enough to save Falwell from near destruction a decade later. At his darkest hour he would have to look elsewhere to save himself, his church, and his university. In doing so, he and son Jerry Jr. would engineer the biggest educational comeback in U.S. history.

4. BIBLICAL BLING

HUNDREDS of millions of dollars poured into the ministries of Bible Belt televangelists in the 1970s and 1980s. But these fortunes would have never materialized without a secular weapon from the North—a Massachusetts marketing outfit begun by a group of twentysomething Harvard grads called Epsilon Data Management. Falwell began using the company in 1976; he was the first televangelist to sign up. When his contributions exploded, other preachers like Pat Robertson, Jim Bakker, Oral Roberts, and Rex Humbard contracted with Epsilon and made a pile, too.

Before Epsilon, Oral Roberts used punch-tape-driven Friden Flexowriters. Billy Graham handwrote every homespun fundraising appeal himself. "You could see the buckwheat flying off the paper," recalls Gaylord Briley, one of the top religious fund-raisers of the era. In a few years Epsilon was doing work for seven of the top ten televangelists in America.

The biggest mailing lists in the world of religion were owned by Catholics; many exceeded several hundred thousand names. But Catholic mail campaigns didn't spend a lot of time espousing dogma. "Catholics never confused faith with funding," says Briley. Baptists, on the other hand, were known for doctrine-heavy content. They used smaller lists whose members were fervent about their faith.

Computerized database marketing turned the late 1970s into an era known as the golden age of direct-mail prospecting. Direct mail was still an almost clandestine medium. You could get away with a lot in a private letter to a prospective donor. The content of such correspondence was rarely exposed to media scrutiny. Falwell crafted his letters with theological abandon, hitting his mortal enemies with blunt force. With Epsilon's help Falwell added urgency to his appeals, pushing his donors to act fast. Epsilon led Falwell to discover that the secret to steady income is consistency; getting lots of donors to give a little, but regularly. Epsilon also taught Falwell that most donor lists contain "compulsive contributors"—usually amounting to 4 percent of the list, says Briley. A charity with, say, 500,000 donors, has a "secondary constituency" of 20,000 potential members who may give even more if asked in the right way to do so.

Epsilon was founded by four junior faculty members of the Harvard Business School who worked out of basement offices writing financial case studies for business classes. One of the four was Hal Brierley, whose fraternity asked him to find a way to automate its 150,000 alumni records. When he couldn't find a company to do it, he and his three classmates saw an opportunity and co-founded Epsilon.

Brierley would go on to pioneer the first frequent-flier program, offered by American Airlines, and to develop customer loyalty programs for Blockbuster, Hilton, Sony, Hertz, and the National Football League. But cofounder John Groman stayed with Epsilon and began working with Falwell after a company staffer paid a call on Falwell's church. Groman has never granted an interview to discuss his fund-raising efforts for the pastor from Lynchburg. "I'm only talking to you because Jerry Falwell died."

Groman was a lifelong Catholic, but it didn't take him long to grasp the fundamentalist subculture.

"Fundamentalist Christians are isolated from the world. They trust their own kind to a fault. If they could they'd build their own cars," he says. "Fundamentalists will always ask you when you accepted Jesus Christ as your personal savior. I learned that if you answered with a general time period, like 'early fifties,' they'd know you were lying. I always answered with the exact date and year."

Groman says that the first thing he had to do was convince Falwell that, with all due respect, the pastor had had no idea what he was doing. Thomas Road Baptist Church was sending out mail pitches by certified postage. That was not only expensive (at one dollar per letter) but dangerous because it forced people to come to the post office to pick up a fund-raising pitch. "I thought he was out of his mind," says Groman.

To Groman's surprise, few people did complain. Over the years Falwell had built a deep reservoir of trust among his flock. His church numbered in the thousands yet he had met virtually every member and was on a first-name basis with hundreds of his church members. He was bringing in about $5 million in annual donations, thanks to a staff of seventy who hand-assembled one hundred mailings a year. There were holiday mailings, pitches for capital projects, and pleas to help balance Liberty's budget and to build new dormitories. Church volunteers sat along rectangular tables sorting, stuffing, and affixing mail labels by hand. Spirtually driven and loyal to a pastor they trusted, they worked long hours and never complained.

Falwell usually included a "premium" in his pitches—something in return for a donation, such as a Bible or an audiotape of a sermon. Groman suggested Falwell take the concept further. Groman and his point man on Falwell's account, Jim Lavin, coordinated direct mail and broadcast spots in which Falwell sold off square footage in new buildings, walls of bricks and brass medallions on classroom doors. "Our biggest problem was people showing up to look for their bricks. We couldn't keep up with all the commemorating," says Groman.

Groman's work applying database marketing principles to Harvard alumni lists had revealed the power of impersonal automation. Direct mail, like television, could be used to create the illusion of intimate contact. Epsilon was one of the first marketers to segment donors by frequency and size of giving. When Groman put someone's name in a letter, it would indicate the person's past giving history. "Donors were never asked to give money," says Groman. "They were asked to pray and decide whether to give. You would get more money by respecting them." A donor's file would be filled with information about them—Groman understood which parts of the file to personalize in the letter and which not to. On some mailings, only donors who had given $100 or more in the past six months would be contacted.

Epsilon expanded Falwell's mailing lists and produced three direct-mail pitches to an average 500,000 targets per mailing per week. Drafts of letters would be written by Falwell and Lavin. Epsilon would subcontract the printing, collating, and assembling to a "letter shop." At its peak, fifteen people at Epsilon were consigned to Falwell's account. Epsilon was paid $20,000 per month plus 8 percent of the mailing budget.

One of the boldest campaigns Epsilon conducted for Falwell was his attempt to raise $5 million by "Miracle Day"—September 24, 1978—on behalf of his university (then known as Liberty Baptist College). In August, at the first chapel service of the school year, Falwell held a rally with nearly one thousand of his students on a grassy field on Candler's Mountain. He did not yet have any permanent buildings for his college; Liberty classes met at a nearby middle school. In the winter the school's furnace kept breaking down, so Liberty students had become accustomed to meeting outdoors. In the rainy season tents were erected, but the area became plagued with mudslides—students dubbed their meeting ground the "Red Sea." In August 1978, Falwell addressed the incoming class, calling on them to help him build a permanent university, preaching about Jericho from the Book of Joshua: "Our world is in trouble today. That is why you are here to train and prepare to minister in a world of more than four billion people who desperately need Jesus Christ. . . . We have gathered on this mountain today for a prayer meeting. We desperately need five million dollars and have come to ask God to supply that need by September 24, which I have set aside as 'Miracle Day.' "[1] Sermons and television spots on the *Gospel Hour* built the suspense in Biblical allegory. The following month, on each of the six days preceding Miracle Day, Falwell made a dramatic gesture. Each morning he drove around the entire eleven-mile circumference of the mountain, followed by hours of prayer. Finally, on Sunday the 24th he drove around the mountain seven times, traveling seventy-nine miles.

Direct-mail pitches work best when they deliver ultimatums—Falwell portrayed the fund-raising drive as a race against the clock. Epsilon's direct mailings went into overdrive, offering a new and unique premium: "Faith Deeds." These were personalized certificates sent to donors who contributed $100 or more to "purchase" a piece of the mountain for Liberty's benefit, but only if done so before the deadline. They were printed to look like official land deeds, while noting that the documents were "symbolic" and had "no conveying authority." Falwell could not print them fast enough. By September 24, the results were in. The campaign had produced not $5 million, but $7 million. Falwell was astounded—it was more money than he had raised from contributors during the entire previous year. "What they bought was a piece of Jerry's dream," says Groman.

A few days after every big televised appeal, Falwell would visit the church mailroom, then report the results to Lavin. "Jim, I hope you're sitting down. We're running eighteen trays!" he'd proclaim. A tray translated to several hundred letters, and Falwell could mentally translate trays to dollars.

Like any shrewd entrepreneur, Falwell knew when to bet the farm. One such gamble was a toll-free telephone number. Lavin says Falwell was the first televangelist to use one. After watching an infomercial that used an 800-number to peddle Ginzu knives, Lavin says he called Falwell to suggest they try it. It would be costly, but Falwell instantly bought the idea. "When Jerry tried something new he'd say, 'If it works, great. If it doesn't we'll call it a test and never do it again,' " says Lavin. Falwell agreed to pay Epsilon's costs to hire a bank of operators and set up a call center. During a single appeal for Liberty in 1980, the center received just over 100,000 calls.

Aside from one-shot appeals like Miracle Day, the most effective direct-mail pitches were threats to cut off the *Gospel Hour*'s airing in contributors' markets. "We'd say that unless we can get friends like you to help us, we might have to kill the broadcast," says Groman. If this sounds similar to "pledge week" on public broadcasting, it is—Groman worked for the Public Broadcasting Service, too. "The executives at public broadcasting would throw up if they knew the techniques we developed for them grew out of our work for fundamentalists."

Money brought in from televangelists was 30 percent of Epsilon's revenue. "The earnings on these accounts were fantastic. The rest of the company was barely making money," says Groman. Epsilon's business from televangelists like Falwell paved the way for it to go public in 1984; it was later sold to American Express for $60 million (today it's a $300-million company).

Besides the savvy of Epsilon, Falwell also had the formidable talent of Jerry Huntsinger. Then forty-five, Huntsinger was a religious marketer brought in after the judge-appointed outside board told Falwell he needed help. A former minister who lived on a farm near Richmond, he had been taking advertising concepts from the for-profit world and applying them to nonprofit religious ventures.

Huntsinger brought a novelist's touch to direct mail. He considered every fund-raising letter a "first cousin" to the short story. "A short story has a problem that seems insurmountable, a sympathetic character that is a victim of the problem, complications, and obstacles, but finally, a resolution." He advised his clients that emergency appeals work best because they give donors a feeling of "excitement at coming to the rescue." He knew to always ask for larger amounts of money from donors than even his clients wanted.

Huntsinger was also a master at fine-tuning the mechanics: the color of the envelope, the position of the address window, which paragraphs to indent, which sentences to underline. He knew how to lure a reader's eye just to where he wanted and how to make it linger just another moment before they either tossed the solicitation in the garbage or decided to send a check.

He had worked with an eclectic mix of clients, authoring mailers for campaigns that brought in millions for Catholic nonprofits. Televangelists were one of Huntsinger's biggest areas of growth, and he knew how to treat his new customers. "Huntsinger had a sliding-glass wall with a well-stocked bar for those members of the clergy who liked a little booze in private," says Briley.

Falwell set up monthly marketing meetings to review how prior direct-mail efforts fared and to plan new ones. They met at a local Holiday Inn around a horseshoe-shaped conference table, where he was joined by Groman, Huntsinger, and about twenty others: staffers from Epsilon; employees of Falwell's television, radio, sales, and marketing divisions; staffers from the data-processing and fulfillment departments; printing and mail-shop clerks. In a room full of male fundamentalists, one person who was hard to miss was

Janice Gleason, a petite blonde with a model's figure. She was a copywriter hired by Groman who could talk—and, more important, write—the language of fundamentalism. Women working for a church and school in central Virginia were either homemakers or, if they did work, held clerical jobs. Gleason's presence alone was a subversive element, which Falwell didn't mind, says Groman.

To anyone attending Liberty's monthly marketing meetings, it was obvious that Falwell had given Epsilon and Huntsinger carte blanche. Huntsinger came to one meeting and detailed the thousands of additional names that he had added that month by swapping out address directories of church members with mailing lists possessed by conservative newspaper and magazine publishers. Huntsinger encouraged Falwell to focus on wedge issues in his mailings, excoriating the feminist movement and attacking homosexual rights, often equating both with the dangers of communism.

As one letter stated:

Dear Friend: I refuse to stop speaking out against the sin of homosexuality . . . I believe that the mass of homosexual revolution is always a symptom of a nation coming under the judgment of God. Recently 250,000 homosexuals marched in the streets of San Francisco. The homosexuals are on the march in this country. Please remember, homosexuals do not reproduce, they recruit, and many of them are after my children and your children. This is one major reason why we must keep *The Old Time Gospel Hour* alive . . . So don't delay. Let me hear from you immediately. I will be anxiously awaiting your reply. P.S. Let me repeat, a massive homosexual revolution can bring the judgment of God upon this nation. Our children must not be recruited into a profane lifestyle.[2]

The sense of impending doom the letter conveyed fit perfectly with Huntsinger's operating credo. It turned a pitch into a storyline (gays on the the march) with sympathetic characters (children) under threat from sex offenders (gay pedophiles). It was an emergency appeal that sought to panic his audience into coming to the rescue. Antigay vitriol of some of Falwell's pitches scored points with his most conservative followers, but they typically raised little cash. "Dreams raised far more money than hateful stuff," says Groman. And plenty of money was coming in. What had started as Macel coming home to a stack of envelopes on the kitchen table had evolved into a half dozen members of the church, all ladies, meeting in the basement of Central Fidelity Bank at 8 A.M. each morning to open the growing pile of contributions. One member always stopped at the post office an hour beforehand, where "third shift" postal workers would have the stack tied by string ready for pickup. It used to take just a morning to open all the mail. As volume grew it would take all morning and some of the afternoon; then the entire day. Thanks to Epsilon, the volume of mail was growing so large in the late 1970s that the ladies from the church simply could not keep up with it.

Falwell soon found a solution: he created a "reading and edit" room on the ground floor of a vacant variety store next to a Lynchburg A&P. In 1979, the operation appeared, at least visually, to be a ladies social. Seventy-five women, mostly church members and the young wives of men attending Liberty, sat and chatted as they opened thousands of letters a day. They would sit down at tables of four, gingerly take off their gloves, primp their hair a little, then begin reading, sorting, and coding the mail. One group did nothing but open correspondence with electric letter openers, zipping open the bottoms of envelopes to determine whether a contribution was enclosed, and if so, whether it was cash. If a flash of green emerged, the money was required to be clipped to its envelope and stacked in a box for special deposit. Letters with checks were sent onto the main floor.

"We worked eight to ten hours a day and could process a letter in under two minutes," says Ann Hudson, then a mail reader. There was "white mail" (first-time writers that came in unattached to any pitch); mail for devotional clubs like "Faith Partners"; and mail sent in BREs (business return envelopes) in response to direct-mail pitches. There were prayer requests, often accompanied by checks or cash, and responses to product pitches Falwell would make on-air for Bibles, gold Jesus First pins, and tapes of choir recitals and sermons. At around 2 P.M. each afternoon, Falwell would call Donald Moon, an accountant he had hired to oversee the operation. "Don, what's the deposit?" Falwell would bark. It ranged from $50,000 to $1 million. Contributions were highest at the beginning of the week, known as "Million-Dollar Mondays."

Downstairs from the reading and edit room Falwell built a parking garage and a secure area with a drop box and a concrete safe. Security guards drove in and picked up deposits in the garage. Falwell always parked his Suburban here; local activists knew what Falwell drove and vandalized his car at every opportunity. "A lot of bomb threats were made against us in those days," says Don Moon. "We spent a lot of time standing around outside as the building was searched, over and over again."

The money brought in by Falwell's direct-mail operations was coupled with a boom in tithes to Thomas Road, which was one of the fastest growing churches in the United States. Conservative Christians were suddenly on the national media's radar screen. *Newsweek* dubbed 1976 the "year of the evangelical"—Jimmy Carter, who had been endorsed by Pat Robertson, had awakened conservative Christians to their own power. But Carter turned out to be a social liberal; conservatives were furious at the thought that they had helped elect him.

Falwell would soon be visited by Warren Phillips, a Jewish Republican who had headed two federal agencies in the Nixon administration; and Paul Weyrich, a conservative Catholic activist who had founded the Heritage Foundation with financial backing from Joseph Coors. Besides contempt for Carter, Phillips and Weyrich were also furious over plans by the Internal Revenue Service (IRS) to yank the tax exemptions of Christian schools who were following federal racial integration standards. Evangelical schools had been flourishing for the past decade; some were founded with the intent of skirting federal desegregation. Weyrich and Phillips met with Falwell (and other pastors with schools), and urged him to gear up his congregation in protest. He refused, believing his church members, and those elsewhere, would be uncomfortable mixing politics with theology. If they had such a desire to do so, Falwell wanted proof.

Weyrich commissioned a $30,000 national poll to see if Falwell (who contributed $10,000 to the effort) was right. A few months later at the Lynchburg Holiday Inn Weyrich released the results of the survey. "It showed not only that people supported mixing politics with religion, but they were chomping at the bit to do so.

After that, Jerry worked with us full tilt," says Weyrich. The cause was as much about money as morality. The proposed tax rules could cause tuition to rise by as much as double at some schools. As Weyrich told author William Martin, "What galvanized the Christian community was not abortion, school prayer, or the Equal Rights Association." What brought pastors and their congregations around the issue was the prospect of being hit in the pocketbook.

Now convinced, Falwell, along with Catholic and Jewish leaders, unleashed a barrage of mail on members of Congress—by one estimate Capitol Hill received 500,000 letters. The correspondence promised electoral Armageddon for any member of Congress who supported the new education rules. Falwell's phone bankers lit up congressional switchboards like Christmas trees, urging members to speak up against the plan. The IRS backed down.

Phillips and Weyrich proved they could unite conservatives of different faiths with a common political objective. They could now turn this power against President Carter, doing so by advancing a common social agenda (prolife, antigay, anticrime, and pornography) and a common economic vision (tax cuts and deregulation). Falwell and his Epsilon-backed direct-mail machine was their obvious choice to lead the effort. A pastor running the organization would give it a bulletproof patina.

Falwell imagined the synergies between this new national political organization and his direct-mail operations back home. The potential to nationally enlarge his fund-raising footprint was staggering, he thought; the equivalent of Magic from Mecca. Legally, they would have to be separate organizations. Functionally, they would grow each other. The free media from voter registration and political mobilization rallies necessary to defeat Carter would be staggering. Falwell's donor rolls would explode.

The Virginia headquarters for the Moral Majority was a small rented office next to a barbecue restaurant in downtown Lynchburg. Its phone-banking operations were run out of a modest brick warehouse twenty-five miles east, in Appomattox. It consisted simply of a floor filled with a forty-cubicle phone bank run by students from Liberty University working four-hour shifts at minimum wage. Clocks on the walls were set to time zones across the United States. Its purpose was to duplicate the success of the IRS campaign, making it appear that a wave of national protest had descended upon members of Congress.

Falwell needed an able captain to open a Washington office and to organize state chapters. Weyrich introduced Falwell to Ronald Godwin, a conservative Christian college president in the Florida panhandle, to be the Moral Majority's executive director. Godwin would create a simple structure, allowing the chapters to be formed on an ad hoc basis. They would raise their own money and appoint their own boards, with little oversight and virtually no authority from Lynchburg or Washington. The idea was to encourage self-starting pastors who shared the vision and could organize voter registration. They would be trained to bring political activism to their own local churches undirected by a central office. Ultimately, it would prove to be the wrong organizing model. "Some of the heads of these state chapters went off the reservation," says Weyrich. "They issued crazy statements that made the whole organization look foolish. It drove Godwin nuts. He had to shut 'em down."

Falwell boasted of the organization's cross section of Catholics and Jews, but virtually every state chapter was run by a Baptist and the entire national board was filled with members of the Baptist convention. As the organization got off the ground, media reports confused Falwell's own hometown direct-mail juggernaut, which had taken two decades to evolve, with the Moral Majority's own fund-raising prowess, which, in spite of Falwell's high hopes, never took off.

Until the founding of the Moral Majority, Falwell and Macel lived in a modest subdivision on Chesterfield Road, an easily spotted home that became a predictable target every time a mailing went out attacking gays and feminists. Falwell's home was regularly pelted by eggs and firecrackers. Falwell had even begun to get bomb and kidnapping threats. Most pastors would have toned down their rhetoric; Falwell was simply emboldened. The attacks suggested to him that he was succeeding against the "enemy." Each day, Falwell literally believed he awoke to a battle zone, and each day was a measure of how far the battlefront against Satan could be moved. Some of his enemies were far closer to home. In 1980 Falwell's newfound political influence caused Bob Jones Jr. to term him "the most dangerous man in America."

Claude P. Brown, an Atlanta trucking-business mogul who sat on the *Gospel Hour* board, privately voiced concern to Falwell about his house being a target. Brown made an offer to buy a property and to donate it to the church. Falwell found an old plantation home built in 1849. It was once occupied by Ferdinand C. Hutter, a former Confederate paymaster. The two-story home, with twelve rooms and a swimming pool, is on seven bucolic acres. Brown bought it in 1979 for $160,000. After giving it to the church, Thomas Road paid for an eight-foot-tall fence and a security kiosk to be built, and put a twenty-four-hour-per day guard on duty.

Falwell was now living life at a faster speed, and he thrived on the energy it required from him. He traveled everywhere by jet and employed a six-person personal staff. On a single day in 1980, Falwell woke at 4 A.M., boarded his jet for a flight to Lansing, Michigan, for an "I Love America" rally; spoke at a luncheon for pastors; returned calls to contractors wondering when overdue payments would arrive; took his jet back to Lynchburg to officiate at a 2 P.M. funeral; made a round of fund-raising calls to cover some of the payments to his clamoring contractors; then flew back to Michigan for an evening service. After the service he stood in a blazing hot auditorium for an hour, signing Bibles.[3] It was not an atypical day for someone who was building a university, pastoring a 12,000-member church, running a national political organization—and fund-raising for all three all at the same time. "The man loved life. He could never get enough of it," says Richard Viguerie.

Yet, the 1980 election proved that what Falwell was best at was winning not so much with real troops on the ground, but simply the threat that they existed. At its peak, the Moral Majority raised a mere $11 million annually, yet Falwell claimed it raised millions more. The organization raised so little money that Falwell soon had to funnel funds raised for his ministries to his political organization. The IRS revoked the *Gospel Hour*'s tax exempt status during the years 1986–87 (and ordered Falwell to pay $50,000 in taxes) for doing just that. Falwell said the Moral Majority registered six million new voters. That would put his outreach cost at less than two dollars per new voter, an impossibly low figure. Even at its peak, the "Moral Majority Report" had a circulation of one million.

Falwell was fond of stating that the weekly viewership for the

Gospel Hour was 25 million. In the summer of 1980, a Falwell associate stated the audience was closer to 50 million. In truth, the number, according to Arbitron, was closer to 1.5 million.[4] Given Falwell's sky-high profile in the presidential race that year, it's astounding to discover that, in terms of audience rankings, Falwell's flagship show came in sixth, with less viewers than Rex Humbard, Oral Roberts, Jim Swaggart, or Robert Schuler.[5] But Falwell was a student of the Civil War. He remembered Jubal Early's trickery in convincing Union forces that Confederate reinforcements were pouring into Lynchburg during that summer of 1864, when in fact a single railroad car buoyed by a cheering crowd was behind the ruse.

On the day after the 1980 election newspapers and television networks were dissecting Ronald Reagan's narrow victory and the defeat of five liberal Democratic senators, and giving Moral Majority voters the credit. Back in Lynchburg, a media mob swarmed a victory rally inside an auditorium at Liberty Baptist College. Network correspondents and reporters from *The New York Times* and *Washington Post* had come to cover a phenomenon they had never before witnessed. As Falwell walked briskly into the rally a band struck up "Hail to the Chief." The place went wild. "It was an awesome and defining moment," says Cal Thomas. "We were no longer the backwoods yahoos who wore blue suits and white socks."[6]

Perhaps so, but less than a year later Falwell would get a reality check on just how much power he wielded. Falwell was at a meeting in Myrtle Beach, South Carolina, when he got a call from the White House. It was Ronald Reagan on the line, saying, "Jerry, I'm going to put forth a lady on the [Supreme] Court. You don't know anything about her. Nobody does, but I want you to trust my judgment on this one."[7]

"I'll do that," said Falwell, overwhelmed that he was being consulted on a Supreme Court appointee by the president himself. The following month, after Sandra Day O'Connor's nomination, Reagan called again.

"Jerry, I've had a chance to talk to her, and my people have, and I can tell you that her views would not disappoint you, and I hope you can help me bring the troops in."[8] Falwell did, calling fellow pastors and conservative pundits. It wasn't so much Falwell, but John Groman and his colleagues at Epsilon (then working for the Republican National Committee) who "credentialed" the relationship between evangelical voters and Ronald Reagan. "The political parties had never really given their members the proper credentials, such as membership cards and bumper stickers," said Groman in an interview. So we created the Ronald Reagan Presidential Task Force, which was really a fan club for Ronald Reagan. We mailed thirty million packages, which was unheard of in prospecting. These were very expensive, closed-face stamped packages, including a seven-page letter inviting people to pledge $120 to the task force. We enrolled over 200,000 people, who paid every month for memorabilia, like an American flag, a lapel pin, a medallion, the first time that premiums of that nature—we called them 'collectibles'—were used in politics."

Falwell's association with the Reagan White House was paying spectacular dividends to his ventures back home. He reported contributions of $110 million in 1985, then $135 million in 1986. He was a regular on *Donahue*, debated nuclear proliferation policy with the prime minister of New Zealand, and met privately with the prime ministers of Israel and South Africa. After a visit to Johannesburg in 1985, he urged Americans to buy Kruggerrands and made his famous attack on Bishop Tutu, saying, "I think he's a phony, period, as far as representing the black people of South Africa." As usual, it drew headlines, and as usual, Falwell backpedaled. Falwell's fame had turned him into a movie critic, too. In 1984 Clint Eastwood called Falwell to ask him whether he'd agree to critique an advance screening of *Pale Rider,* the only overtly religious film Eastwood had ever done. Eastwood played the title role—a gunslinger who saves a small community of miners from a greedy corporate mining company trying to take over the town. The "pale rider" arrives on a white horse as a little girl reads from the Book of Revelation, a reference to the fourth horseman of the Apocalypse, "Death." Falwell never went to see movies, so Eastwood offered to rent a local theater and shut it down for the evening. Falwell saw it and gave his blessing to the film.

Falwell's high-flying profile with Republican leaders and the Moral Majority attracted a new kind of contributor: the superdonor. Texas oil billionaire Nelson Bunker Hunt had given millions to the Moral Majority. Now he was becoming one of Liberty's biggest contributors, along with life insurance moguls Arthur Williams and Art DeMoss, cotton magnate Bo Adams and a wealthy Pennsylvania poultry farmer, Don Hershey. They saw Liberty University as a logical component of a conservative Christian renaissance. As large as their donations were, they could never keep up with Falwell's expanding vision for a 25,000-student university and his dream to build the largest church in America.

The problem was that Falwell was spending his newfound millions as fast—or faster—than they came in. In the summer of

1985, he hired 325 workers to construct twelve new dorms on campus and to add an entire floor to the sprawling DeMoss building. Falwell was buying television time in new, expensive markets, too. Then, in March 1987, he suddenly got an opportunity to reach his colossal goals faster than he ever dreamed possible.

Until that moment, the idea of Falwell taking over a Pentecostal denomination would have been a laughable heresy to anyone who knew him. Falwell had nothing but contempt of Pentecostalists' habits of snake handling and speaking in tongues. As he once put it, "You can talk in all the tongues you want, but do not do it at Thomas Road Baptist Church; it confuses things. I want our people to know what we are saying . . . God is not the author of confusion."[9] Yet, there he was in a Palm Springs hotel that morning, speaking to Jim Bakker, listening to a small parade of sins and then a blockbuster request: "Jerry, I want you to take over PTL."

The Bakker affair has spawned books, television specials, movies and even an off-Broadway show. It was known as *Gospelgate* and revolved around sex, religion, fraud, adultery and bribery. Falwell described his own role in the affair as spiritually motivated. In truth, his rationale for taking over Bakker's PTL ministry was a business decision—perhaps the worst he ever made.

Falwell knew the numbers. In 1978, the Bakkers turned what was a tiny rustic campground into Heritage, a 2,300-acre Christian theme park that brought in $126 million annually just eight years later. Some six million people visited Heritage each year, more visitors than DisneyWorld. They had built the 504-room Grand Heritage hotel, a 3,500-seat outdoor amphitheater, and the PTL television studios, which beamed the Bakkers' shows by satellite to an estimated audience of 12 million viewers a week. Some 500,000 of those viewers were PTL "partners"—high net-worth donors. A single campaign aimed at the partners, offering them lifetime vacations at Heritage, had reaped $158 million alone.

Jim and Tammy Bakker had started their career as the original hosts of Pat Robertson's *700 Club*. The show had been started by Robertson to keep afloat a defunct UHF station Robertson used to air the show. It cost $7,000 a month to operate, so the Bakkers asked for 700 listeners to call in and pledge ten dollars per month to cover costs. They wound up raising far more. After a falling out with Robertson, the Bakkers moved to North Carolina and started their own network and similarly formatted show called the *PTL Club* in an abandoned furniture store. The folksy talk show was a huge success.

That is, until the spring of 1987, when rumors, probably started by Bakker rival Jimmy Swaggart, began to circulate involving Jim Bakker having sex in a hotel room with a church secretary. Falwell got wind of the alleged affair from fellow pastor D. James Kennedy. The two began working with a small group of pastors who wanted to contain the crisis, if there was one. Falwell soon became the group's leader and believed that the rumors were true. He saw the makings of an opportunity. Seeing the magic worked by Epsilon, he believed that, in the right hands, even more money could be raised from the PTL's massive donor base, but only if Bakker were out of the picture and the PTL's reputation were restored.

Falwell's explanations to the press, of course, revealed no such financial motivation. Neither did Bakker honestly reveal his reasons for turning to Falwell. Bakker was using Falwell as a bulwark against Jimmy Swaggart and others whom he believed were trying to seize control of PTL. Falwell portrayed himself as a paternalistic white knight. "Television ministers don't have many friends who will confront or correct them," said Falwell. "I was doing for Jim and Tammy Bakker, and for PTL, exactly what I hoped my fellow television preachers would do for me." Of course, Falwell wasn't a friend of Bakker's; he barely knew him. And he demonstrated almost immediately that, once he had control of the PTL, he had no intention of relinquishing power.

Falwell was again at the center of a storm. After the news was announced that the old PTL board was to be replaced by a new one—packed with Falwell allies—Falwell was swarmed with attention. He got calls of congratulations from Vice President George Bush, Billy Graham, and Sen. Jesse Helms. At a press event held after the board's first meeting, three hundred journalists attended, worthy of a presidential press conference.

After just three meetings of the new PTL board, two things were clear: (1) Bakker's financial misdeeds were far greater than he initially revealed, and (2) Bakker believed that Falwell had abruptly turned against him. Bakker was already plotting to reclaim his ministry with the help of yet another board. He would soon send Falwell a telex, stating that he wanted Falwell to resign and to turn the ministry over to a new board dominated by fellow Pentecostalists. "I will not fight you if you ignore my wishes," Bakker wrote, "but I must let you know that what you are embarking on will truly start what the press has labeled a 'holy war.'" Falwell soon discovered what may have touched off Bakker's suspicions. He claimed that an electronic sweep of the PTL's headquarters turned up a surveillance device in the boardroom.

Word of the Bakkers' bizarrely lavish lifestyles were leaking to the press. They had used church funds to build an air-conditioned doghouse and buy his-and-her Rolls Royces. They blew ministry money on bizarre whims, like the day the Bakkers reportedly spent one hundred dollars to have several trays of freshly made cinnamon buns sent to their hotel room just so they could enjoy the smell, with no intention of eating them. Ultimately, it wasn't the cars or cinnamon buns that did Bakker in, but a bribe of a church secretary named Jessica Hahn.

In revealing his infidelity with Hahn to Falwell, Bakker neglected to mention that he had paid her $265,000 to keep the affair quiet or that the person who made the payment was Richard Dortch, Bakker's self-appointed successor, board member, and substitute host of Bakker's *PTL Club* television show. Falwell's response to Bakker's telex wasn't exactly accommodating. At Falwell's urging, his new board fired Dortch and then revealed some of the embarrassing financial details that were coming to light in the board meetings, including the fact that the Bakkers had earned two million dollars in bonuses and salaries from PTL the previous year.

The Bakkers returned fire, making two consecutive appearances on *Nightline* in which they accused Falwell of trying to steal their ministry. Falwell held a press conference the next day, denouncing them. "I don't see any repentence there," he said. "I see the self-centeredness. I see the avarice that brought them down."

Falwell was able to raise $22 million to help pay off creditors, but that wasn't nearly enough to keep the organization afloat. He was soon forced to file for bankruptcy and sell off PTL's assets. Bakker and Dortch would go to jail, but with the perverse satisfaction that Falwell would not be in control of the empire they built—it had been destroyed.

Falwell had taken over PTL to save the ministry and hoped to reap the spoils for doing so. He failed on both fronts, yet would not admit personal responsibility. Instead, he explained his role as the product of theological machinations. He couched his colossal failure, in which he presided, as God's will. Said Falwell:

> I am convinced that God led me to Heritage in 1987 . . . Heritage had become the Mecca of the "prosperity theology" movement. God wanted it terminated. I now clearly see that Jehovah God gave me the very unpleasant and painful, but necessary, task of exposing and calling a halt to this modern Sodom and Gomorrah.[10]

It is unlikely that Falwell suspected, as he claimed to, that a major scandal at Bakker's single ministry could touch off across-the-board drops in donations among other, unrelated ministries. The audiences for these televangelists did not change; the core constituencies of their ministries did not leave. Second, the Bakker scandal coincided with a period of escalating costs of television time. Programming blocs that had once been a purchase of last resort (Sunday mornings, for example) became a hot commodity that secular media outlets could charge more for because of booming competition. "It was an auction market," says Groman. "Evangelical fund-raisers turned into greedy little bastards. They were all competing with each other to get the best time slots."

Religious broadcasters who could no longer afford the prices stopped buying time. That produced a boomerang effect. People who could no longer watch broadcasts of their favorite pastor simply stopped donating money to his ministry. Finally, if Falwell really did forsee that a single scandal at a fellow ministry would unleash such negative fallout across all other ministries, why didn't he also try and save Jimmy Swaggart's ministry, which imploded just after the Bakker disaster over Swaggart consorting with a prostitute? By November 1987, the backlash against televangelism was in full throttle. Not every ministry was affected—Billy Graham's organization actually reported an increase in contributions—but most others were noticing sizeable declines in giving. Many reported dips in sales of religious books and a drop-off in seminary enrollments. For the collection plates of churches in the south, especially in Texas, Oklahoma, and Louisiana, the timing was awful. The oil industry was entering a recession and the real-estate market was in the dumps. The financial ripple effects between the scandalous press of Swaggart and Bakker combined with the job losses and rising gas prices diminished contributions. Churches that had financed construction of new facilities using bonds could not keep up payments.

Falwell resigned his PTL leadership and returned to Lynchburg. But it was too late. In that single year, he faced a $40 million deficit. The PTL debacle would soon cost him far more.

5. Magic City

A MONG Jerry Falwell's inner circle of benefactors were real-estate tycoons, retailing moguls, and apocalyptic novel-ists. They all shared his dream of a West Point for the faithful. But it was the head of this inner circle, a billionaire from Palm Beach, Arthur L. Williams, in whom Falwell discovered a personal and ideological soul mate.

Williams grew up in Cairo, Georgia (pop. 9,239) and had the twang to prove it. His father died when Williams was twenty-one. A short time later he began selling life insurance to earn some cash on the side while he coached high-school football full-time. Williams brought his young team to a championship in three years by push-ing them to the brink. When team members said, "I can't," Williams would call them into his office and wallop their backside three times with a giant wooden paddle. After the pain subsided, they would yell, "I can!"

Williams's insurance career took off when he started A. L. Williams and Associates in 1977 with eighty-five agents. They convinced customers to switch from whole life to term insurance with the slogan, "Buy term and invest the difference." Ten years later his sales force of part-time agents had grown into an army of 150,000, selling $93 billion in policies annually.

Williams met Falwell in the heyday of the company's growth in 1982. A conservative Methodist, Williams was a big believer in Christian education and thought it was about time to contribute some of the wealth he was amassing to try and advance the world of Bible-based academe. He was invited to come to Lynchburg and meet Falwell by Mark DeMoss, son of Liberty benefactor Arthur DeMoss and Falwell's chief aide. Williams visited Thomas Road Baptist Church on Sunday and went to lunch with Falwell to talk about growth plans for Liberty.

Williams shared Falwell's passion for football and conservative politics. Like Falwell, he had come from a small town in the south, was a passionate Christian, and made it big on a national stage. Both felt that secular universities like Princeton and Harvard were polluting America with students who were, in Williams's words, "fence sitters and mealymouths." Students from liberal schools had lost touch with God and lacked "mental toughness," he said. Elite universities spent too much time thinking about the world, not changing it. "If you want to win in these United States, you gotta stand for something," said Williams.

Like Falwell, Williams carried a chip on his shoulder when it came to the pedigreed culture of the Ivy League. He believed their business schools had little to offer.

> I thought at one time in my life that you had to be smart to win. I used to know smart people who dressed so pretty, talked so pretty, and used these big words. They just intimidated me, and I said to myself, "Art, you can't ever be that good. Why don't you just throw in the towel and go back to coaching football for a living?" Well, I found two things out about smart people. One is that it's almost impossible for a smart person to win in business because smart people spend their whole lifetime figuring things out. They're always trying to find an easier way, a quicker way. Another thing about smart people is that they just don't get around to doin' nothin'. They see somebody like Art Williams and say, "He can't do it."[1]

In 1989, Williams did it, and did it big. He sold his company to Primerica, netting some 19 million shares of stock in the deal. In 2007, *Forbes* pegged Williams's worth at $1.8 billion. His home is on a stretch of beachfront that sells for $114,000 per linear foot with neighbors like Bavarian Prince Hubertus Fugger, Jimmy Buffett, and conservative talk-show host Rush Limbaugh.

Palm Beach is a long way from Lynchburg. Yet, Falwell and Williams became close, sometimes talking daily. Williams and his wife hosted Falwell and Macel aboard the 140-foot *Lady Angela*, a yacht named for Williams's wife. They shared lunches and dinners together. Falwell sent Williams his sermons in the mail; he'd listen to three or four of them a day. Williams flew in to attend Liberty

Flames football games when the team was at home. Falwell and Williams also shared admiration for Ronald Reagan's principles of conservative economics. Not that Falwell practiced any of them. In his own business ventures, Falwell borrowed and spent money like, well, a liberal Democrat.

Williams and others in Falwell's inner circle were only vaguely aware of the dramatic falloff in contributions after the Bakker affair. Even if they knew about the 30 percent drop in annual contributions, it's unlikely they could make up for such losses. Yet, when the moment came when Liberty's very life hung in the balance, it was Williams who would commit the staggering amount of money needed to keep the university alive.

Falwell used capacious leverage to pull off an economic hat trick: he kept his empire growing as income declined. In the aftermath of the Bakker-Swaggart scandals and the escalating costs of television time, he embarked on a borrowing binge lasting a decade, using his church as collateral eleven times, and piling up nearly $100 million in debt. Contributions declined, yet Falwell continued buying land and constructing dozens of dormitories and classroom buildings, erecting Liberty's basketball arena, football stadium, and a colossal student center so fast that students wondered whether he was trying to beat the Second Coming. It was a remarkable feat given Virginia's then-antiquated laws governing church holdings and finances. Every time Falwell's church took on a substantial loan or acquired property, he was required to get permission for the transaction from a district judge. To get around these rules he used other entities like the *Gospel Hour* to hold and grow his ministries.

All conservative Christians consider betting a vice, but Falwell's accumulation of debt was probably the biggest gamble of his life. He was wagering that he and Jerry Jr. could find ways to repay short-term loans even though Liberty was a long-term investment. Falwell was also betting that contributions would one day return to their mid-1980s levels. Until then, he would face a financial conundrum: the school could not become self-sustaining until its enrollment was large enough, but that growth would only come when campus programs were distinctive enough to lure tuition-paying students in the first place.

The lion's share of Falwell's spending was fueled by another kind of bettor: bond underwriters. The PTL disaster might have decimated income from Falwell's national television broadcasts, but buyers of church bonds seemed unfazed by the fiasco. Underwriters who sold the bonds didn't want to turn away business from the pastor of the fastest-growing church in America, which Thomas Road had been named a few years earlier. How many Lynchburgers had become fixtures on *Donahue* and *Larry King Live*? How many were consulted by presidents on Supreme Court nominees?

One financier eager to strike a deal with Falwell was Willard E. May, a former fundamentalist preacher who had been introduced to Falwell by a Lynchburg loan broker. In the 1980s, May reigned as king of the one-billion-dollar Texas church bond market. The little-known Texan was chief executive of AMI Investment Corporation, which operated from a 26,000-square-foot headquarters in a high-rise in Amarillo. With salt-and-pepper hair and a gentle, reassuring drawl, May welcomed clients to his office, decorated with hand-carved rosewood furniture and a turn-of-the-century Limoges tea service.[2] He would soon undertake Falwell's biggest ever bond issue.

Church bonds were financial instruments whose existence was common knowledge to pastors but mostly unknown on Wall Street. They've been used since the 1930s to build many of America's megachurches, giving pastors the money they needed to construct new sanctuaries, rectories, and parking lots for their schools, and the cash to build prayer halls and libraries. The bonds were snapped up by altruistic churchgoers looking for high returns helping institutions they believed in.

The bonds typically deliver 8 to 14 percent yields, as much as triple the return of a bank-issued certificate of deposit. They are not rated by services like Moody's and don't appear on exchanges. They are exempt from SEC registration because they are issued by nonprofit organizations. Unregulated, and with no protection by federal insurance, a default can be triggered by a drop in collections or, say, a pastor who becomes ensnared by a sex scandal. Defaults are rare. From 1954 to the late 1980s, underwriter A. B. Culbertson Trust Company produced 2,400 issues. In that period a mere twenty churches fell into default.

Willard May had been a trader at Culbertson but left to start his own brokerage in Amarillo, Texas. May's underwriting standards were looser than his competitors—a fact that should have been a red flag. His pitch was that his bonds could be protected by a May-owned insurance company. This was something virtually unheard of in the church bond business, but it worked. By the late 1980s, May racked up $400 million in issues for three hundred churches. He even took on outside investors like savings and loan fraudster Charles Keating Jr., who acquired a $4 million stake in an AMI subsidiary and extended $50 million in credit to May.

May had begun planning a bond offering with Falwell for

Thomas Road in 1987. The following year Falwell sent a direct-mail pitch to members of his church, promoting the investment and its delivery of interest rates at between 9.5 and 11.5 percent. He included May's toll-free number in the letter. Falwell also promoted the bonds in the Moral Majority's newsletter, with a full-page story lauding May and his companies. It was quite a success: 2,200 investors bought $32 million in bonds. May was so thrilled he promised to donate $1.5 million toward the new 12,000-seat football stadium Falwell was building.

In 1989, the Texas insurance commission shut down May's bond insurance company, alleging that he was unauthorized to offer such coverage. A few months later Texas banking regulators accused May of mismanaging several million dollars of church and corporate bond funds held in AMI's trust company by putting them into unauthorized, high-risk investments (according to May, the investigation was later dropped). The SEC took over the trust company, declared it insolvent, and claimed all of its possessions.

May was left with one asset: a lifetime air pass from American Airlines that AMI spent $265,000 to purchase for May's use. The pass let May and a companion fly first class on American, anywhere, anytime, forever. May began another business: using the air pass to escort executives to Europe, charging them for the first-class seat at a reduced rate. He even checked their bags and drove them to the airport.

May had also taken Falwell for a ride. Among the items that fell into regulators' hands when they seized May's trust company was the deed to the Thomas Road Baptist Church, provided to May as collateral for the bond offering. The federal government now owned Falwell's church, the headquarters of his television network, and about 130 acres of his land.

By now, Falwell was getting some sorely needed legal advice from a new attorney working as staff counsel to the Gospel Hour—twenty-nine-year-old Jerry Falwell Jr. He had graduated from law school just a year earlier but had no plans to begin a career at his father's church or university. Jerry Jr. intended to practice law in Lynchburg and enhance his income with some real-estate ventures on the side. Why would his father's famous religious-educational-political empire need the skills of a kid just out of law school? Jerry Jr. had no reason to doubt his father's success. In the year Jerry Jr. became a lawyer, his father placed second behind Reagan in a *Good Housekeeping* poll as America's most admired man.

Jerry Jr. wasn't the only one in the dark about his father's ventures. When Falwell disbanded the Moral Majority in 1989, he made no mention of his simmering problems back home. He explained in a press conference that the Moral Majority succeeded in defeating liberal members of Congress, put a God-fearing Christian in the White House, and reestablished a moral agenda for the nation. "Mission accomplished," said Falwell. By all appearances, things seemed fine back in Lynchburg. In fact, Falwell had made a flurry of announcements about Liberty's quickly growing athletic programs, in particular his football team, the Liberty Flames.

Falwell knew that the gridiron is the holy grail of recruiting. As the Moral Majority was disbanding, he hired Sam Rutigliano, coach of the Cleveland Browns from 1978–84, to take over Liberty's football squad. He gave Rutigliano a $100,000 recruiting budget and began building a three-million-dollar football stadium. He would spend liberally on a dozen more athletic departments, eventually establishing eighteen Division One programs. The cash from bond proceeds and tuition was being voraciously consumed. Jerry Jr. soon learned why the school's operations budget, including money for sports programs, faculty payroll, and mundane expenses like utility bills, was falling short each month. The school was simply running out of money.

Jerry Jr. looked for a means to make up the shortfall. He sat in his North Campus office and pored over a list of Liberty's real-estate assets. He did some calculations based on their square footage, then called his father and went down the list, tallying up the value he could offer as collateral for short-term loans on the properties. They were worth perhaps $50 million, he thought. In the following few months Jerry Jr. would succeed in drumming up a half dozen loans of about the same value from banks who had worked with Liberty in the past.

Next, Jerry Jr. looked over the notes his father made during conversations with George Rogers, Liberty's chief financial officer. He examined the revenue lines of the church and school. Had any shown growth in the prior year? Two had: Liberty's distance learning program and its Home Bible Institute. Jerry Jr. believed they could boost sales by offering financing for the two programs. He called Household Finance Corporation (HFC) in Chicago, who agreed to help the Falwells. *Who could be more trustworthy than Bible students?* HFC executives thought. Falwell promoted the offer nationwide on the *Gospel Hour*. Students could now finance their $1,200 Bible study tuition by paying just twenty-five dollars a month for forty-eight months. For every student who signed up, HFC would front one thousand dollars to Liberty. Within weeks thousands of new students enrolled by mail. "The growth was extraordinary. It seemed like the answer," said Jerry Jr.

Not for long. The easy financing attracted itinerant students and less-than-committed Christians. Many soon lost interest and stopped making payments. "Household Finance thought that if you take a Bible course, you probably have pretty good credit," says Jerry Jr. "They weren't checking these people out at all. They gambled that these buyers would be far less a credit risk than simply finding people in a phone book." In a matter of months, two-thirds of the new students had defaulted. The Falwells had escrowed 30 percent of the loans as a safety net, but the fund was rapidly depleted. They would soon lose the tuition from their distance learning courses and Bible study program, and ultimately be on the hook for $16 million.

"Don't these folks know we're the ones who'll be stuck with the bill?" fumed Falwell.

Mark DeMoss, who had introduced Art Williams to Falwell, was stunned when Jerry Jr. told him about the HFC defaults. The twenty-seven-year-old DeMoss, who closely resembles actor Rob Lowe, was Falwell's chief aide and his spokesman. Reporters from the Lynchburg and Richmond papers were bombarding DeMoss with unpleasant questions about Willard May's flameout. How big a hit would Jerry Falwell Ministries take? DeMoss, like Jerry Jr., was beginning to sense a financial catastrophe in the making. DeMoss deflected the queries, stating he was confident the May case would have little impact on Liberty, but he had met privately with George Rogers, whose views were not as innocuous. He told DeMoss that diminishing contributions, combined with the Willard May bond debacle and the HFC defaults, could cause a deficit that year of over $30 million.

Falwell had just turned fifty-six. It was close to the age his father had died. Lately, he had taken to making references to the day he'd no longer be present to promote his spiritual empire. DeMoss saw an opportunity to corral the typically short attention span of his boss into a longer, more serious conversation. Meetings with Falwell on campus rarely went beyond an hour: phones rang for Falwell wherever he went, and he always took the calls. DeMoss sensed Falwell was still in some denial about the deteriorating financial state of his school and church. It got DeMoss to thinking: Why not get his boss to confront these issues by holding a summit billed as a meeting to plan Liberty's future? DeMoss confided with Jerry Jr. about his plan and broached the idea to Falwell; he agreed. The retreat would last just two days. It would focus on strategic planning and honestly assess Liberty's financial state. It would be billed to its attendees as a discussion to strategize how Falwell's enterprises would survive him. The real question, of course, was: Would they survive at all?

It was a forty-five minute drive to the Hotel Roanoke, a Tudor-style gem in a town some Virginians still call Magic City. The nickname derives from the meteoric growth Roanoke experienced when the railroads transformed Roanoke from a farm town to a small city in the 1880s. The group consisted of Falwell, Jerry Jr., DeMoss, Rogers, and four mid-level managers from the *Gospel Hour* and the university.

They began over an early morning breakfast in a hotel suite anchored at one end by a large conference table. The white-haired Rogers, Liberty's éminence grise, ran down that year's expected profit-and-loss statements, clutching the papers tightly as he spoke. The biggest item, contributions to the church, had dropped for the second year in a row, to $36 million. Liberty was netting about $4 million from tuition income, but that would be entirely consumed by debt service. The cost to broadcast the *Gospel Hour* on two hundred stations across the country had risen to about $12 million; very little of this expense was being recouped by contributions. If all this weren't bad enough, the specter of being liable for some of the Willard May bond debt and HFC default was looming large. *This is incredible,* thought Jerry Jr. *How could money be this tight?* Falwell had issued dozens of "crisis" direct-mail pitches that year, warning that Liberty faced financial doom, but some in Falwell's inner circle had thought he was exaggerating the threat. Even Jerry Jr. had suspected his father overstated the peril. He no longer did.

Rogers was followed by DeMoss, who scheduled Falwell's trips and decided who got on his schedule. As DeMoss described his job back then, "I didn't have great authority, but I had a lot of influence." DeMoss felt it was time to junk the *Gospel Hour.* It would not be easy arguing for the demolishing of what had been the engine of growth for Falwell's enterprises since before DeMoss was even born. DeMoss knew that he could not win with a head-on criticism of Liberty's crumbling financial foundation. Instead, he would try a flanking action, arguing that radical cuts were needed to preserve Falwell's legacy.

DeMoss put Falwell's television ministry in the crosshairs. "Liberty is no longer a fledgling school," he began. "It has reached maturity. The *Gospel Hour* birthed it, paid for its mortgage, and helped recruit its students. But at this point we're spending a million dollars a month on airtime. What are we getting for this?" DeMoss gazed down at charts Rogers had prepared. They showed outlays for the television network plummeting compared to its revenues. The *Gospel Hour* was not even close to paying for itself.

"There are thousands of universities in this country. How many of them have a national television network?" asked DeMoss. "We're paying one hundred and four people to sit around and come up with new ideas, like televising Liberty football games. I love the Flames. But running these games isn't producing any money for us." Then DeMoss raised the specter of a post-Falwell future. "We need to think about what happens when Doc is no longer around. With all due respect, the reality is that when Jerry dies, the church will go through a tough time. The ministries will struggle. The television network won't have a chance. But the university can survive." DeMoss turned to Falwell. "The university can outlive you, Jerry."

Falwell looked at Jerry Jr., who nodded his head and said, "I have to agree. We should narrow our focus and make Liberty the priority now. This school is our future." A long, silent pause followed. Falwell looked down, blinking fast as he always did when his mind ran in high gear. He was absorbing the words of DeMoss and his son, the two youngest staffers at the table. They would be around to see Liberty succeed, if it did. But Falwell knew that besides drastically reducing his visibility, the cuts would hit Liberty's recruitment efforts hard. Most students still found out about the university from advertisements on the *Gospel Hour*. It was how Becki, Jerry Jr.'s wife, had first learned of Liberty.

Falwell stiffened his lower lip, bending his mouth into a frown. "Well, Mark is right about all this. Television has always been at the heart of our commission. We've always found a way to sustain it. But we can't sustain it by bankrupting ourselves. I guess the question is, How many stations do we cut?"

"I think we've gotta roll back the whole network, nationwide, and just leave a few stations running the *Gospel Hour* locally in Virginia for now," said DeMoss.

Falwell was deflated, but he was not surprised at the drastic medicine proposed by his own team. "Let's do it." The *Gospel Hour*'s national television broadcast was soon pulled from nearly two hundred station slots across the United States, remaining on a mere five stations in Virginia. The cuts would save the Falwells some $10 million a year. Rogers was shocked by the way Falwell so easily capitulated. It was the first time he ever witnessed his boss cutting anything. DeMoss's strategy had worked.

Next, the Roanoke group took up a matter Jerry Jr. had been researching for the past month: changing the business structure of his father's church and school. Liberty was a subsidiary of the church, which in turn was owned by the *Gospel Hour*. Hostile creditors could claim assets belonging to the church or television network. The university, which was already incorporated as a separate nonprofit, would take on the $60 million in debt thus far accumulated by the *Gospel Hour* to build Liberty. The university, in effect, would buy itself. This corporate sleight of hand would protect the church and force Liberty to shoulder its own debt.

Downsizing the *Gospel Hour* made other cuts more palatable to Falwell and Jerry Jr. In the coming months, they would lay off five hundred employees across Falwell's ministries, cutting perhaps another $14 million. They slashed the recruitment budget for the online education program ($12 million), put 2,000 acres of Candler's Mountain land on the market ($4 million), sold the church's Israeli-made jet ($2 million), abolished Liberty's wrestling program ($70,000), and stopped publishing the *Fundamentalist Journal* ($200,000).

Falwell knew he could soon be liable for a portion of the $32 million raised by May (about $16 million of which was collected by Liberty), who was the subject of a widening SEC investigation. But it didn't worry Falwell because he had staked his hopes on the fact that Lynchburg's city council had green-lighted another bond issue. He would sell $60 million in state-sanctioned, tax exempt bonds that would not be due for thirty years.

Until he could get his hands on that money, he would have to figure out another source of short-term cash. Jerry Jr. suggested they could put up one of their last, and most critical, pieces of real estate as collateral. It was fifty acres of land known as "North Campus," which included the offices of both father and son. After a flurry of phone calls to executives at Little Rock, Arkansas–based Stephens Inc., a deal was struck. Stephens, the largest off–Wall Street investment house, who had taken Wal-Mart public, would provide a short-term loan to Falwell for $6 million. The loan would be paid off by the $60 million in coming bond proceeds.

Much of this emergency financial maneuvering was caused by Falwell's unfortunate habit of acquiring loans from local lenders—banks and small businessmen, mostly—which amounted to financing long-term assets with short-term borrowing. Falwell believed he could survive the wipeout in contributions brought on in part by the Bakker fiasco yet continue building Liberty by banking loans like the one from Stephens. He expected that donations would soon return to their mid-1980s level. They never did.

In the midst of this struggle Liberty received a visitor who buoyed the spirits of Liberty's brain trust and reminded them that, even though their school was coming apart at the seams, its profile remained high. The campus had already been visited by the big stars of conservatism: Oliver North, Jesse Helms, Steve Forbes, Ronald Reagan, Phil Gramm, and Newt Gingrich. On May 12, 1990, President George Bush joined the list, delivering the school's commencement at the prematurely named Willard May Stadium. It was the first time in nearly a hundred years that a sitting president had visited Lynchburg. Falwell and Macel met Bush Sr. aboard Air Force Two after the chopper alighted on Candler's Mountain. Falwell sat and bantered with Bush as the Secret Service checked the route to the stadium. Falwell had gotten a haircut for the occasion and mentioned to his barber, a mason named Jimmie Martin, that the president was coming to visit. Martin asked Falwell to get an autograph, so Falwell took along his barber's mason Bible for Bush to sign. "It'd mean a lot to Jimmie if you'd sign it," said Falwell to the president. When Falwell and Macel left from Air Force Two, Bush's entourage lagged behind. A photographer captured the moment the Falwells stepped out of the chopper all by themselves, appearing as president and first lady. Falwell had the photo blown up and hung in his office ever since. The symbolism was not subtle; it was the first image visitors saw when they came to visit him.

Willard May would soon be hit with a six-count grand-jury fraud indictment. Falwell concluded that the long overdue $1.5 million the former pastor had promised would never materialize. After Bush's convocation May's name quietly disappeared from the stadium.

Falwell would have to face the fact that some of the $55 million in short-term debt was now coming due, and there was no way to pay it. To avoid what might become a domino effect of campus property foreclosures, Jerry Jr. suggested restructuring the loans.

He worked out an agreement with Christian Mutual Life Insurance to refinance the $55 million with a massive, taxable bond offering put together by Kemper Securities, an Illinois investment bank. Christian Mutual had worked with Kemper on similar deals. Kemper was so certain there would be buyers that it promised to buy any bonds that went unsold. That pledge would be tested a few months later, when it turned out that Kemper suddenly faced a very unreceptive market. There were very few buyers interested in buying debt from a fundamentalist university in Virginia, no matter how famous its leader was. In November 1990, Kemper phoned Falwell with more bad news. Not only could they not sell the bonds, they believed that there was justification in not fulfilling the pledge to buy the bonds themselves, as they had promised. It was an extraordinary turn of affairs; father and son were furious. Falwell would later tell Jerry Jr. that the day Kemper backed out of the financing was one of the two worst days of his life. The other was when Falwell's mother died in 1977.

Falwell sat down to discuss the matter with Jerry Jr., who said, "Dad, the bottom line is that they reneged on their obligation to us. We oughta sue 'em." The Falwells did sue Kemper, but an arbitration panel ruled against Liberty on what amounted to a technicality. So Jerry Jr. hammered out yet another agreement: Liberty would repay the debt it owed to Christian Mutual with the $3 million in annual profits from Liberty's online program, then grossing about $20 million annually.

Christian Mutual agreed, but as always, it was a short-lived reprieve. Falwell had been waiting over a year for the go-ahead on another bond proposal—the $60 million, tax-free issue that the city had already sanctioned. The plan had been legally challenged by two advocacy groups representing church-state separation, sending the case to the Virginia Supreme Court. In January 1991, the court ruled that Liberty was indeed, as the advocacy groups had argued, a "pervasively religious" institution. As such it could not issue the bonds. Without these bond proceeds, the Falwells had no way to pay off the $6 million owed to Stephens Inc. and already past due. Stephens had held off foreclosing, expecting that the bonds would sell. When the court decision came down, Stephens referred the defaulted loan matter to their bond counsel, the Little Rock–based Rose Law Firm, who seemed to be in no mood to negotiate with Falwell. It foreclosed on Falwell's North Campus property and put it up for sale.

The foreclosure forced Falwell into the humiliating position of having to sell his own office. He carted his belongings himself to a new, isolated site on a hill overlooking Liberty's football field. It was the old Carter Glass Mansion, which Liberty had bought a decade earlier. The North Campus building would be sold over the Thanksgiving holiday and force the relocation of dozens of classrooms, 200 students, and 100 employees to Liberty's main campus. There was one silver lining: the 200 students who lost their rooms found space elsewhere on campus because the *Gospel Hour* cutbacks of the previous year had knocked down Liberty's residential enrollment from 4,400 to 3,400.

For the first time, Jerry Jr. and his father had been evicted from their own property. It was a frightening experience that threatened to be repeated. They now presided over a banquet of bitter IOUs: the restructured debt owed to Christian Mutual ($55 million), the collapse of the HFC student loan program ($16 million), Willard May's bond meltdown ($13 million), and the loan due from

Stephens ($6 million). There were too many creditors to count. The future of Liberty, if it had one, looked mighty grim.

Falwell would need another short-term savior, and very fast. Falwell was staying late into the night at his office, praying and spending hours on the phone. Who was he talking to? It later turned out to be two former Liberty fund-raisers, Jimmy Thomas and Daniel Reber, who ran a lucrative direct-mail outfit just outside Lynchburg. They had read about Falwell's financial problems and had a plan to help.

Thomas and Reber would form a nonprofit entity called World Help to perform a financial miracle. They would use the nonprofit to wipe out $29 million of Falwell's debt by buying what Falwell owed at a discount. In November 1992, their nonprofit spent $2.5 million to buy $12.6 million in loans from Willard May's defunct subsidiary, allowing Falwell to reclaim the deed to his church. The following year, they paid $3 million to assume the $16 million in debt owed to HFC. For the 2,200 who had bought Willard May's bonds, who got about fifteen cents on every dollar of theirs, it would be a bittersweet remedy.

Falwell announced these gifts by casting Thomas and Reber as financial good samaritans who leveraged everything they owned to make the bailout possible. It was probably the biggest whopper Falwell ever told. The money did not come from Thomas and Reber, but from the Rev. Sun Myung Moon's Unification Church. It was a deal almost certainly brokered by Ron Godwin, who had left Falwell's organization in 1986 to go to work as a senior vice president at the *Washington Times,* only to return to work with Falwell in 1999. There was good reason to keep secret the source of the money. Besides the embarrassment of accepting money from

Moon's church, theologically at odds with fundamentalism, there was the chance that if creditors knew the deep pockets of Moon were involved, they may not have settled for such a deep discount.

Moon, who shared Falwell's anticommunist leanings, got little beyond a photo op with Falwell for the deal, but he didn't mind. Moon was grateful for some crucial advice Falwell gave him years earlier. The two had met at a conservative confab in 1981, the year the *Washington Star* went out of business. It was Falwell who suggested to Moon he start a conservative newspaper to compete with *The Washington Post*. Moon launched the *Washington Times* in 1982.

Communism had been defeated in 1989, but with the election of Bill Clinton three years later, Falwell found a new enemy. The depth of Falwell's animosity toward Clinton, whose wife had served at the law firm which foreclosed on the building housing Falwell's own office, might be measured by a video Falwell helped distribute called *The Clinton Chronicles.* Falwell was still in the hole for some $60 million. Yet, he still found time to promote the project, first by sending a direct-mail solicitation seeking $40,000 to fund its production. The low-budget 1994 attack video would make filmmaker Michael Moore blush. It alleged that Bill Clinton sanctioned major drug trading in Arkansas and was responsible for murder. Falwell produced an infomercial for it in which a person identified as an anonymous journalist, shielded in darkness, was interviewed by Falwell. The "journalist" linked several murders to Clinton, saying he feared for his own life. Falwell replied, "Be assured, we will be praying for your safety." It later turned out that the silhouetted figure was Patrick Matrisciana, the conservative Orange County filmmaker who produced the video. "It was Jerry's idea to do that . . . he thought it would be dramatic," he said[3] (Jerry Jr. disputes Matrisciana's account). The *Gospel Hour* had been heavily downsized, yet the video still managed to sell some 150,000 copies.

A month after he began touting the video, Falwell faced a new threat: this one from academe itself. Liberty's bond contretemps had punched some big holes in the school's creditworthiness, causing concern at the Southern Association of Colleges and Schools (SACS), a regional accreditation agency. In June 1994, SACS put Liberty on "warning" after learning of its bond defaults. In 1996, SACS changed Liberty's status to "probation." If Liberty didn't soon find a way to alleviate more of its debt the university would lose accreditation. That would spell certain death. Falwell knew he had only months to turn Liberty around.

Falwell would now employ a new tactic to keep his school alive: fasting. He announced he would go on two 40-day fasts, publicizing them as a fund-raising bid to save Liberty. He went on the first fast in July, returned to his normal diet for a month, then began the second fast in September.

Art Williams knew how fond Falwell was of banana pudding, chicken fingers, and sausage gravy. He knew that if Falwell was fasting, things at Liberty were worse than he realized. He had been told by DeMoss and others about Liberty's ballooning debt, but had made no decision whether, or how, he would help. His concern was that if he bailed Liberty out on this one-time basis, the school could find itself in the same situation a decade later. Falwell's weight loss weighed on Williams; he wondered what Falwell would try next.

A few days after the end of Falwell's second fast, one of

Williams's private planes flew into Lynchburg. Aboard was a lone courier holding a plain brown envelope. The plane touched down at Falwell Airport, a private airstrip run by Falwell's cousin Calvin on land once part of the original parcel bought by Hezekiah in 1850. The courier was then driven to Falwell's office in the Carter Glass Mansion. "I'm here to deliver this to Reverend Falwell personally," he said to Jeanette Hogan, Falwell's longtime secretary. Falwell and Elmer Towns emerged. Falwell opened the envelope and felt his heart skip a beat. Inside the envelope was a check made out to Liberty University for the sum of $27 million. It was to be used exclusively to wipe out half of Liberty's debt.

"Let me touch it," joked Towns.

"Nobody touches this, I'm taking it to the bank," said Falwell, grinning. A few months later, Williams took on another $25 million in debt. "We sailed through the next accreditation meeting without a hitch," said Towns.

Williams's $52 million of munificence would have a price. The deal allowed Williams to become a kind of George Steinbrenner at Liberty that fall. Falwell had consented to a complete audit of the school and to be unconditionally bound by the results. In the fall of 1996, Williams's team flew into Falwell Airport. The group included four accountants and Williams's own chief financial officer. They met and collected documents at Liberty, then returned to a conference room at a nearby Sheraton. They laid out the documents in a conference room: profit-and-loss statements, payroll reports, admission tallies, and recruiting budgets.

They put a dollar figure on what each faculty member cost the university, followed by a second dollar amount based on a calculation of how much they earned for Liberty. They figured out what it cost to offer each course, and how much Liberty made or lost on it. They put an income/expense figure on every major, every school, every janitor at Liberty. This was blunt capitalism being applied to a religious enterprise grown by debt and held together by the sheer force of Falwell's own personality. In short, it was no way to run a business.

Williams's team completed the audit in four weeks, then one of Williams's folks called Falwell. "Jerry, you should probably leave town. We're going to recommend some cuts and send out notifications by the end of the week." Falwell said he understood, and would abide by their decisions. Based on the audit numbers, Williams's team recommended cutting one-third of the teaching faculty. That Friday, for example, Elmer Towns had thirty-six full-time teachers at the school of religion, where he was dean. On Monday he had sixteen. Secretaries and a deacon were told to leave. Some jobs were doubled up. "We called it Black Friday," recalled Towns.

In a written report given to Falwell and Jerry Jr., Williams's group stated that part of the reason for Liberty's ramshackle finances was Falwell's habit of spreading himself too thin, fundraising without focus, and an overreliance on diminishing returns from Falwell's much shrunken television ministry. A consistent problem was that when large donations came in to, say, Falwell's youth programs, they were often deposited in the church's general fund, allowing them to be spent elsewhere. Falwell would draw on them for expenses unrelated to the projects they were raised for. He saw no contradiction in such decisions. In his eyes, his church, university, seminary, and television network were all the same mission.

Falwell realized that the Williams report conveyed some of the same concerns he had heard at the meeting in Roanoke. He now needed to give his undivided attention to Liberty. This is what would be required to wipe out its remaining debt, build an endowment, and create the juggernaut of Christian education he and Williams had dreamed about for fifteen years.

But first, Falwell and his son had a bone to pick with Thomas Jefferson.

6. RIGHTEOUS BROTHERS

THE late author William Styron wondered how Virginia could produce both Thomas Jefferson and Jerry Falwell. Perhaps a greater wonder is how much Jefferson and Falwell had in common, at least when it came to building a university.

Jefferson created the University of Virginia (UVA) in Charlottesville in the 1820s with public funds and private borrowing. He used the Roman Pantheon as the model for his centerpiece rotunda, flanked by pavilions suggesting small Italian villas. They were adorned by Corinthian pediments and Chinese latticework. His "academical village" was a work of intentional bricolage; most of its construction materials came from Charlottesville or its surrounding forests. Jefferson wanted to use mahogany for the front doors of his faculty residences, which faced the school's great lawn, but when informed of the price he used Virginia pine and feather-brushed the lumber instead. When he resorted to imported materials he found ways to bring it into the country cheaply. He commissioned hand-carved capitals of Carerra marble to top the columns of his pavilions but dodged the high import duty for the work under the pretext that UVA's educational mission should exempt it from such usury. Jefferson had himself helped to enact the tax.

Falwell never aspired to such lofty academic design, but like Jefferson, he was a charismatic idealist who believed that the teachings of his school were crucial to the future of the republic. Both had enjoyed the peak of their power years earlier and constructed their respective universities as retirement projects (Falwell had begun Liberty in 1971, but didn't make it the focus of his ministries until after the Bakker-Swaggart scandals unfolded). Both were masters at lulling backers into thinking that their schools' financial conditions were never as bad as they seemed.

Jefferson and Falwell founded their respective schools in central Virginia believing they served an unstated mission: preserving the culture of the South. Jefferson referred to Virginia as "my country"; believing that the southern way of life was superior to that of the north. To him, slavery was an "agrarian virtue." Falwell saw Liberty as an antidote to the poisonous liberal college culture spawned mainly by big cities of the north. He believed his campus would anchor his students in Southern family values like attending church and raising children in a traditional family structure. Jefferson and Falwell even watched the progress of their universities from similar vantage points: Jefferson spied on his workers by telescope atop Monticello; Falwell monitored Liberty's expansion from his headquarters on Candler's Mountain. In the end, both wanted to be remembered as educators. Falwell considered Liberty his pre-eminent legacy. Jefferson ordered his headstone to note three accomplishments (president was not among them): author of the Declaration of Independence, builder of the University of Virginia, and author of Virginia's Statute for Religious Freedom.

Jefferson, a deist, was immensely proud of the Virginia statute. Its delineation of the dangers of governmental sanction of religion was so precise that much of the opening section of the Bill of Rights is crafted in language borrowed from it. Having vanquished the British, Jefferson believed the next great threat to the fledgling democracy—at least in Virginia—was the Anglican church. Taxes were collected on behalf of the church by Virginia's colonial government. Religious tests were held for public office seekers. It was illegal for anyone other than Anglican ministers to preach on the street. Jefferson's statute for religious freedom was passed by the Virginia legislature in 1786 to "disestablish" the church, which it did. But the statute's sanctions and those of succeeding laws put a stranglehold not only on the Anglicans, but on all Virginia churches for the next two hundred years.

Under this jurisprudence the state of Virginia confiscated vast tracts of unused church property, known as "glebe lands." Church holdings were limited to ten acres (though cities were later allowed to enact higher limits); churches could own a maximum of $50 million in property. It was one of the reasons the Falwells had to set up the *Gospel Hour,* the Liberty Broadcasting Network, and the university as their own corporations. No church in Virginia could incorporate itself. Jefferson's aura around these laws was powerful—no church in Virginia had ever successfully challenged them. Until 2001, when Jerry Falwell got the real-estate opportunity of a lifetime.

The property was an 880,000-square-foot cell-phone plant owned by the Ericsson Corporation. A vast complex, equivalent to eighteen football fields, it was next door to the Liberty campus. That year Falwell got wind that Ericsson would be vacating the property and planned to sell the building. It would be a perfect place to base a law school—the one Falwell and Liberty's board had been dreaming about. A school of law would add immense prestige and credibility to Liberty. Its legal eagle graduates would fight the culture war on secular ground—in American courtrooms. Falwell's problem was that he had no place to put it. The only campus location with the space required was the upper floors of the sprawling DeMoss Center. That was fine for classrooms, but the floors could not support the massive weight that books from a law library would impose.

Falwell's desire to obtain the Ericsson property faced two small hurdles. He didn't have the money to purchase it, and even if he did, church laws made it illegal for him to buy it. Falwell asked Jerry Jr. what, if anything could be done. Jerry Jr. surprised his father when he said that he had been contemplating a legal challenge to the church laws for years, but the time never seemed right.

Jerry Jr. asked a fellow Falwell legal ally to weigh the odds of winning such a suit. He called Mat Staver, the head of Liberty Counsel in Orlando, Florida, a kind of conservative ACLU Falwell had been working for years. Staver and his wife Anita had litigated dozens of religious cases and won most of them. More important, they were outsiders. "There's a mentality in Virginia which says, 'We're the oldest colony. This is where America was created. Thomas Jefferson and James Madison lived here,' " said Staver. "We weren't from Virginia, so we didn't have those concerns."

The Stavers flew to Richmond and spent days poring over judicial precedence on Virginia's religious freedom cases going back to the Revolution. They concluded the case was a slam dunk. If challenged, they predicted, a court would find that the Jefferson-era laws discriminated against the First Amendment rights of churches. Staver quickly filed suit to challenge the constitutionality not of the statute itself, but the succeeding laws which applied the incorporation ban and land restrictions. The key defendant was Clinton Miller, chairman of the Virginia State Corporation Commission. *Falwell v. Miller* would never gain as much attention as *Falwell v. Flynt*—the 1988 case which strengthened protections for parodies of public figures—but in Virginia it would be more consequential.

Staver told Falwell he would be victorious, so Falwell put in a $10 million bid for the Ericsson property. There was more at stake than just the law school. A building that size would be able to consolidate all of his ministries, he thought. The university had begun in a room in the church. With the new property, the church could move into a wing of the school.

In April 2002, the Stavers and the Falwells got the news they expected. A federal court in Lynchburg ruled that the provision in the state constitution which banned churches from incorporating was unconstitutional under the equal protection clause of the First Amendment. Within days Thomas Road became the first church to incorporate in Virginia since the Revolution. Within a year, some three hundred more Virginia churches followed suit. In October, the court ruled again in the Falwells' favor. It agreed that Virginia's statutes relating to church property ownership were unconstitutional on the same grounds. A later ballot measure to amend the state constitution would be required, but until then the courts would not enforce the 200-year-old laws.

That month a Liberty board member who knew David Green, chief executive of retailing giant Hobby Lobby, got word that Green's foundation was shopping for a worthy religious organization to which it would donate a building it had bought in Chicago. Would Falwell be interested in the property for his law school? The offer put Falwell in an uncomfortable position. His purpose in seeking the Ericsson building, which he had no guarantee of obtaining, was to base his law school on campus and to consolidate his ministries. He had no intention of starting a satellite school.

On Valentine's Day, 2003, Falwell traveled to meet Green at Hobby Lobby headquarters in Oklahoma City. It would have been easy enough to call Green and graciously decline the gift. But Falwell had something else in mind. Ericsson had accepted Falwell's bid of $10 million, but called him en route to Oklahoma City to say the company wanted to postpone the sale for two days. That was good news for Falwell; he still had not found financing to buy the building. Falwell arrived in Oklahoma with two rolls of schematics tucked under his arm. Over lunch in Green's office, Falwell declined Green's gift, then unfurled the rolls of paper. "Jerry had laid out his whole vision on those drawings," says Green. Falwell regaled the Hobby Lobby founder with the mission of the law school, which he likened to a Christian West Point. It would graduate soldiers who would rush the courthouses and inject a Biblical grounding to the understanding of American law. "Some day, our law school students will be on the Supreme Court," said Falwell. Falwell told Green that the Ericsson building was an opportunity not only to build this legal citadel, but to transform his church and school.

The following week Green made the purchase, then drew up a lease that would allow Thomas Road to occupy the building for one year at a price of ten dollars. At the end of that year the foundation would donate the building to Falwell's enterprises, valuing the gift at several times higher than they bought it, reflecting the millions in conversion costs the Falwells poured into the building, including $20 million to create a new sanctuary for Thomas Road.

Falwell asked Green to give the property to the church, not the school. He did this to cast his church as a doctrinal watchdog over the school. Liberty owed its birth and early existence to subsidies from the *Gospel Hour,* controlled by Falwell. "Any time they start teaching something we don't like, we cut the money off," Falwell once said. "It's amazing how that changes philosophy." But over the last decade, as enrollment boomed, Falwell phased out most of the *Gospel Hour* subsidies. Liberty's tuition took on the lion's share of its own operating costs. The school was heavily in debt, but finally had financial independence.

The Ericsson property reconfigured Liberty's borders into the shape of a bulging arrowhead at the base of Candler's Mountain. At its forward tip the Falwells would construct a new, 6,000-seat sanctuary for Thomas Road Baptist Church. The doors of the church would open out to "Main Street," a kind of indoor arcade lined with Biblical murals and handmade tapestries leading to two student restaurants, an indoor track, basketball courts, administrative offices, classroom space, and the new, 120,000-square-foot law school, where Mat Staver would become dean. In the summer of 2006, Thomas Road celebrated its fiftieth anniversary at the new site. In just a few short years, Falwell had succeeded in knocking down landmark laws to expand his church; added nearly one million square feet to his university, and founded a law school. In the midst of this he found time to conceive and break ground on a luxury retirement community near the top of Candler's Mountain. He imagined a child could begin school at his K-12 Liberty Christian Academy, attend Liberty University, pursue a career in Lynchburg, and then retire at Liberty Village. When Jerry Falwell died the following year, he had broken ground on every level of this cradle-to-grave vision. Jerry Jr. and Jonathan were now managing most of the day-to-day affairs of the school and church. By 2006, Falwell had set the stage for his own departure.

G OD took Dad and split him right down the middle," says forty-two-year-old Jonathan Falwell, now senior pastor at Thomas Road. "He gave his business acumen to Jerry Jr., and his speaking abilities to me." Jonathan, the younger of Falwell's two sons, is a golf nut and a devotee of all things high tech. He also has a streak of voyeurism. Beneath Jonathan's desk is a digital archive of three million photos sitting on four terabyte-size hard drives. He has personally snapped most of them. There are thousands of behind-the-scenes moments of his father, mother, brother, sister, and children at weddings, birthdays, vacations, and anniversaries; candid shots of Michael Milken, Rupert Murdoch, and George W. Bush Jr.; images of Falwell on the back of a Harley-Davidson motorcycle driven by Lynchburg police chief Charles Bennett; Falwell meeting with Mel Gibson and Paul Lauer, marketing genius behind *The Passion of the Christ*; vacations to Sonoma County wine country, Pebble Beach, Lake Tahoe, and DisneyWorld; tens of thousands of photos of his father conversing with members of Congress, with foreign leaders, and with members of the Supreme Court; and thousands more taken at scenes of religious events, meetings, and political rallies over the past decade.

Jonathan spends a lot of time on the "grid." From his cell phone he can access four different versions of the Bible. Like his father, he reads passages from Oswald Chambers's classic, *My Utmost for His Highest,* but does so late nights on his home computer, after his wife Shari and four kids have gone to sleep. He sometimes rolls through as many as twelve to fourteen meetings a day at his office on the second floor of the Ericsson building, just down the hall from Jerry Jr.'s office. By his own choice Jonathan's office is spartan and smaller than his brother's. A Bible sits on a small, dark oval table next to the window with two chairs underneath, where he sometimes ministers to visitors. From his window you can see the mythic points of the Peaks of Otter.

The lamp by his desk is shaped in the figure of a duffer in mid-stroke. Over the years he has also taken a swing at some entrepreneurial ventures. Not far from his Liberty office is the spot on Candler's Mountain road where he opened a restaurant in 1998 called At the Hop, investing 60 percent of its start-up costs. Jonathan's partner in the venture was Christos Carroll, a deacon at Thomas Road. Jonathan's appearance is remarkable for how little he looks or sounds like his famous father. Square-jawed and blue-eyed, with a bristling wave of red hair, he has virtually no trace of twang, and preaches twice the speed as his dad's measured cadences.

His diner didn't last long, but an earlier venture is thriving. Transamerica Duplicators, a video production shop Jonathan founded in 1990, brings in as much as three million dollars in annual sales. Video duplication companies are high-margin ventures, especially with the kind of low overhead Transamerica operates under. Jonathan's company is run out of a modest, white cinderblock building in a low-rent, rural stretch of land along the edge of the Lynchburg airport. Jonathan says he "walked away" from the venture to spend more time in his pastoral duties in 1994. Well, sort of. The Virginia State Corporation Commission lists Jonathan as the company's current president; Carroll as vice president. Recent IRS filings by Jerry Falwell Ministries show that it steered one million dollars to Transamerica from 2002 to 2006. Recent filings make no mention of Jonathan's ownership of the company.

Jonathan got his first taste for how closely the local press scrutinizes anyone with the name Falwell when, at age nineteen, the *News & Advance* penned a story about Jonathan driving a BMW registered by his father to the *Gospel Hour* (presumably to reduce insurance premiums). His father had bought the car at cost from a generous Tennessee car dealer. Jonathan was in his second year at Liberty and not an employee of his father's ministry at the time. More serious was the attention he got a few years later, when Jonathan was entangled by the IRS, who accused him of selling a Moral Majority donor mailing list to the National Republican Congressional Committee for $50,000. It was a fund-raising bid for Liberty and the *Gospel Hour,* he says.

Jonathan has always been his father's fiercest defender, once even going undercover for him. In 1984, he accompanied his dad to the Democratic National Convention in San Francisco, where his father was a speaker at a conference on family values at the Hyatt on Union Square. Several hundred protestors, many waving cartoon caricatures of Falwell, showed up in front of the hotel to boycott Falwell's appearance. Jonathan didn't fully understand the venom being spewed at his Dad. He wanted to confront their anger, but surreptitiously, so he infiltrated the demonstration by posing as a photojournalist. As he descended into the crowd to photograph his father's foes, things got out of hand. "A group of anarchists showed up and started kicking over newspaper stands," says Jonathan. "All of a sudden it turned into a riot." Jonathan was pushed around in the melee, but escaped injury and arrest.

The next day his cover was blown when he accompanied his father to a radio appearance. In the green room were two guests for an upcoming segment. One was Jack Fertig, a drag performer known as Sister Boom Boom. The activist had been at the demonstration and instantly recognized the young photographer. "You mean, you're his SON?!" gasped Boom Boom, referring to the elder Falwell as if he were the antichrist. Fertig converted to Islam in 2001, and now works as an astrologer in San Francisco.

In 1987, Jonathan attended the National Religious Broadcasters Convention, where Arthur Williams would make a wildly entertaining speech about faith and business. He had his camera with him, as he always did when he traveled with his father. As he walked around the convention hall, he spotted Jimmy Swaggart and John Ankerberg huddled together in a private, intense exchange. Jonathan snapped a photo of the two. "That was the exact moment John was telling Jimmy Swaggart about Jim Bakker's infidelity," says Jonathan, cracking a grin. He sold the shot to a handful of news magazines. It would be one of the defining images of the Bakker affair.

While Jerry Jr. was away at law school in the mid-1980s, Falwell mused to reporters that Jonathan might take over as Liberty's chancellor one day; someone else might take over his pulpit at the church. That plan changed when Jerry Jr. began legal work for the *Gospel Hour* and Jonathan joined his father's church as assistant pastor in 1994, at age twenty-eight. Like Jerry Jr., Jonathan stayed out of the spotlight in his early years at the ministry. He took on administrative roles and only began preaching in 2005, when his father's heart troubles began.

When Jerry Falwell preached at Thomas Road, he cocked his head and spoke at angles to his congregation. His stayed behind his pulpit, occasionally watching its built-in count-down screen to know when it was time to pause for a segue necessitated by the national feed telecasting the service. Falwell's wide, beige pulpit is still there, but Jonathan hovers near it only long enough to glance at the clock. He paces in long strides from one end of Thomas Road's Broadway-size stage to the other. His hands are in constant motion, framing thoughts with his palms up, forming his hands into U's as if holding invisible binoculars. Behind him is a 300-person choir decked out in purple robes, backlit by a three-story blue screen, with the words, "Not I, but Christ" towering over them. On most Sundays white-haired church deacons sit regally in thronelike chairs on either side of the pulpit. They listen poker-faced to musical performances that run from light country to Christian pop. Accompanying them is a fourteen-piece band, accented by a bald trumpeter wearing a green bow tie. It's a colorful warm-up to Jonathan's high-octane sermons, which he delivers with far more exigency than his dad. In the five months following Falwell's death, some 1,100 new people joined Thomas Road. That brought in a record take from the collection on Sunday, October 7, when the church reeled in some $170,000 on that single day. The average take for the week is $200,000.

His passion for gadgets led him to launch a series of sermons in the summer of 2007 called, "iTruths: Life Lessons for the iPod Generation." He began the eight-part program by rolling out an eight-foot iPod on stage, whose screen glowed with Biblical passages. He is working with Apple to create a new division of iTunes called iTunesChurch, where a portal will zip you to a repository of archived Thomas Road services, music, devotionals, and shows carried on the Liberty network. That summer, under the burning lights of Thomas Road's TV-friendly sanctuary, Jonathan built a one-story house on stage out of plywood to parallel spiritual growth with home construction. He made wacky allusions to Sherlock Holmes and four-legged chickens to convey lessons about Biblical commitment.

Unlike Garland Falwell, Jonathan has never heaved mustard-gas canisters out of his car window. But a bad-boy streak is there, often in the form of attacks on the media. In a 2007 column he skewered reporters for "twisting" Ann Coulter's reference to Sen. John Edwards as being gay. He drew headlines with a direct-mail piece, which attempted to counter critics of his father's infamous comments about 9/11, in which Jerry Falwell blamed gays, feminists, and pro-choicers for the attack. "Satan has launched a hail of fiery darts at dad," wrote Jonathan, referring to media outlets that ridiculed his father's remarks. "He was my dad. I will defend him to the death."

Jerry Jr. defends his father's actions on most matters, too, but does so with greater aplomb. Like Jonathan, he bears little resemblance to his father. With dark hair tipped by some early gray, he has a farmer's tan and the demeanor of an unflappable country lawyer. His father favored black suits and crimson ties; Jerry Jr.'s style is business casual with a twist. He's almost always in a navy jacket, dress shirt, khakis, no tie, and his trademark Crocs (of which he has six pairs). Jerry Jr. is low-key and innately friendly. When he challenged his dad he did so obliquely. In one meeting, Falwell bluntly described Liberty's athletic programs and law school to a reporter as "platforms for our message." Jerry Jr. offered a more nuanced take: "The church has its mission. Our business is education."

Jerry Jr. earned an undergraduate degree in religious studies at Liberty. He met his wife, the former Becki Tilley, an attractive brunette, when she was thirteen. A few years later, when Jerry Jr. was a second-year law school student at the University of Virginia and Becki was a freshman at Liberty, they began dating. "She was interested in an M-R-S degree," jokes Jerry Jr. (code for "husband-huntin'," he says). After Liberty he trekked north to Charlottesville to attend law school at the University of Virginia, whose busts of alum Robert F. Kennedy Jr. in its law library would not be popular on the Liberty Campus. When Jerry Jr. returned to Lynchburg on class breaks he took Becki on horseback-riding dates atop Candler's Mountain. Liberty turned out to be a good place to find a husband; Becki and Jerry Jr. were married in October 1987, and bought their Bedford farm the next month. Becki's family tree includes ancestors with ties to George Washington and Robert E. Lee. Her father is a mobile-home mogul from North Carolina and a longtime Liberty contributor. For years she managed an upscale dress shop in Rivermont, but admits she's a bargain hunter at heart.

"Most of the kids I went to law school with went on to work at practices in Washington, New York, or Atlanta," says Jerry Jr. "I suppose I could have done something like that, but I felt a duty to come back home." When he returned to Liberty and discovered the impending financial doom the school faced, he realized he had another duty: to survive. "I always had a strategy in place if, by chance, everything blew up," he says. "That's why I kept my hand in real estate." In the last decade Liberty has watched some $80 million in retail development sprout around it thanks to Jerry Jr. As a buyer, a broker, and a dealmaker, he has had his hand in nearly every new acre of that development. Most of these deals have been done on Liberty's behalf; the university and church accrued dozens of gifts and made strategic purchases of land numbering into the thousands of acres over the years. Jerry Jr. convinced his father to buy a swath of barren hillside beside Wards Road on the northern border of the campus at $100 an acre, for example. Jerry Falwell Ministries sold the land less than a decade later for nearly ten times that price to Lynchburg's first Wal-Mart. Jerry Jr. has made some profitable transactions near campus for himself, too, like a stretch of land around Candler's Station, which he bought for $75,000, then sold four years later for close to one million dollars.

Just four days after his father's death, Jerry Jr. leaned back in a patio chair, his back to the horizon of picturesque, rolling hills surrounding his home, known as the "Falwell Farm." It was dawning on him that he'd be spending a lot less time on real-estate deals. The lush, 83-acre property is in Northeastern Bedford County, in the heart of a small valley first settled in the mid-1700s. Until the week of his father's death, Jerry Jr.'s role in his father's ministry had been pivotal, but unseen. His father was Liberty's public persona; Jerry Jr. was the university's operational guru.

"I guess I'm going to be a lot more visible now," says Jerry Jr., wearing the expression of a man contemplating a root canal. At

Liberty's commencement the previous day, Jerry Jr. sat next to Newt Gingrich, waiting for his cue to take the podium. Jerry Jr. turned to Gingrich, confessing how rusty he is in front of a crowd. "I really don't have much practice doing this stuff."

"You know, with someone like your dad, practice wouldn't have helped," said Gingrich. "He sucked up all the attention in the room, no matter who he was with."

Near Jerry Jr.'s 1918 home are paths cut into his forested property by Jerry Jr. and his son Trey. The two, occasionally with Falwell Sr., mounted four-wheel ATVs and raced up the trails. Their destinations included a small Civil War graveyard, where the crumbling gray headstone of Confederate Lt. Col. William Wilson is still visible. On another trail is a nineteenth-century cabin, inhabited until recently by a hermit. A bolt of lightning set the structure ablaze, leaving the cabin deserted again. Building runs in the family genes. Trey has already got a summit picked out on his father's property where he wants to build his home. "Why would I want to live anywhere else?" he says, gesturing to the Blue Ridge Mountain skyline.

Jerry Jr.'s home office is dominated by a relief map stretching over the entire wall behind his desk. Its elevated ridgelines inch up from the surface alongside major population zones, colored in yellow. His father posted maps in his office to grow his church; Jerry Jr. uses his to grow Liberty's real-estate empire. "We made a good team," he says.

B ESIDES Jerry Jr. and Jonathan, there is a third force who guided Falwell in his final decade: Liberty's chief financial officer,

Ronald S. Godwin. "My own little career beats the fool out of fiction," says Godwin, sixty-seven. He is a mountain of a man; a six-foot-two-inch image of Vladimir Lenin whose steely gaze makes one feel like a target being lined up on rifle sights. He is rarely in a tie, favoring neatly tailored gray suits over a snow white turtleneck.

Godwin is a veteran of the Religious Right who did two tours of duty with Falwell. The first was as executive vice president of the Moral Majority in the 1980s. Falwell bonded with Godwin, whom he admired for rising out of an obscure existence in the Florida panhandle to become president of two Christian schools. They traveled together everywhere. As Falwell disbanded the Moral Majority in 1987, Godwin was approached by an official at the Unification Church to see whether he might be interested in working for Moon. The job was senior vice president for New World Communications, the Unification Church–backed publisher of the *Washington Times*. "They offered me a ton of money and the chance to travel around the world." It was an easy decision for Godwin, but a tough one for Falwell, who sat in Godwin's office in tears when Godwin broke the news.

Before his stint with Falwell Godwin had graduated from fundamentalist Bob Jones University with a master's degree in organizational management. Moon's staffers believed Godwin had empathy for religious owners, and could be trusted. But Godwin did not completely trust them. He says he wrote a clause into his contract stating that if any member of Moon's church tried to convert him, he'd be entitled to a $500,000 penalty. He never collected. Godwin started work in his new Washington office days later, but for the next few months he was constantly reminded of his old job. Sitting near him were three IRS agents who believed

Godwin had kept a second set of books while working at the Moral Majority. Each week several boxes of newly requested financial documents would arrive and the agents would pore over them. "It was total nonsense. There was never a second set of financials," says Godwin.

Godwin became an ambassador for the *Washington Times* and a roving efficiency expert for the giant constellation of Moon's enterprises in real estate, hotels, and restaurants. He swooped in on Moon-owned operations to analyze productivity and to suggest ways to squeeze profits, he says. He got to know all of Moon's children and attended their birthday parties. His budget was prodigious. For a 4,000-guest *Washington Times* banquet, Godwin rented the Great Hall of the People, the giant edifice on the western edge of Tiananmen Square.

Godwin had returned to Liberty after a twelve-year absence, becoming Falwell's chief financial officer and spokesman in 1999. He had left on the brink of Liberty's near-destruction and returned on the cusp of its miraculous rescue. When he returned he was rich, but his personal life was a shambles. Falwell was alone in his sympathy for Godwin. To some faculty members hiring Godwin was blasphemy. He was a twice-divorced single man who had spent the last decade working for the Moonies. One administrator likened him to Slugworth, the character in *Charlie and the Chocolate Factory* whose true loyalties—to Willy Wonka or his competition—were unknown. "In our subculture, hiring me was a very outrageous thing to do," says Godwin.

If Godwin was surprised to be rehired, he was shocked to discover the tenuous standing of Falwell himself on campus. The years of living in financial quicksand had taken its toll with some members of Liberty's thirty-five-member board. Liberty had been put on probation by the Southern Association of Colleges and Schools for a second time. The SACS review committee was concerned not just about Liberty's debt but the amount of Falwell's power in administrative decision making. Why was the school being run by both its president and chancellor? Some Liberty board members believed the school was recovering in spite of Falwell, not because of him.

Two years before Godwin returned, its then president, A. Pierre Guillermin, had resigned. Falwell and the Liberty board chose John M. Borek as his replacement. Prior to joining LU, Borek, then a consultant with LU, had been chief financial officer at Georgia State. More important, he had served on thirty accrediting committees for SACS. With the colossal gifts from Art Williams in place, Borek was the point man to get Liberty back in good standing again with SACS.

Borek succeeded. His star was rising at Liberty just as Falwell's was falling. "Jerry felt unwelcome on his own campus," said Godwin. "Borek took the place over and marginalized Doc. There was even talk about moving Doc out of the mansion, across the road into some double-wide trailer. He had been wounded by all these financial problems and Borek took huge advantage of that." For his part, Borek says, "Some may have felt this way, and it may have been for their personal gain or status with Dr. Falwell, but it is not true."

Falwell made a prescient countermove: he convinced the board to appoint Godwin as executive vice president and Liberty's chief financial officer. Falwell had saved Godwin; now Godwin would save Falwell. He drew up a list, much like the one he brought to breakfast with Falwell each morning, only this one had names of those he considered Borek's base of support: Liberty administrators and faculty Godwin identified as "enemies." It did not take long to whittle it down, he says. "Let's just say there's no one left on it."

From that point on Godwin became Falwell's Karl Rove. They traveled together constantly, often in motor homes—at one point three RVs had been donated to Liberty. Whenever a destination was two hundred miles away or less they'd climb aboard one of the rigs, often driven by Liberty police chief Randy Smith. On one trip to Richmond in 1999, Godwin sat reading an article by Jim Collins in the *Harvard Business Review*. It explained how corporate executives achieve their "BHAG" (pronounced bee-hag), an acronym for "Big Hairy Audacious Goal." Godwin handed the article to Falwell, who furrowed his brow as he read it, then burst out with a belly laugh. "I love it." Falwell certainly did, using the term regularly at events with students and faculty. On the night before his death, he delivered an impromptu, five-minute talk to kids at the Liberty Christian Academy. "If you want to change the world, find your BHAG!" he intoned.

Godwin often got Falwell out of jams, but he couldn't always save his boss. It was Godwin who accompanied Falwell to the worst media appearance of Falwell's life: a segment on Pat Robertson's *700 Club* two days after September 11, 2001, in which he blamed pagans, abortionists, gays, feminists, and lesbians for the attacks. Godwin does not mince words on the subject. "I blame Pat for that September 11 interview and all the trouble it got Jerry into," he now says. "Pat knew better than to ask a question like that. Jerry had done thirteen other interviews that day. When Jerry came on the show, it was just two preachers talking. Pat did the interview and walked away. He did nothing to help fend off the attacks we received for the next three weeks." Falwell's sentiments became a signature paragraph in every obituary.

In the last few weeks of his life, Godwin's office became Falwell's refuge. Godwin's ground-floor suite sits next to a campus parking lot, where Falwell would park his SUV and then sit in the chair, laying in wait. When a student or faculty member walked by, Falwell would punch his wireless remote, setting off the whoop of his truck alarm. Falwell would double-over in laughter as his victims sprang four feet in the air, then turned around with a scowl. Liberty's chancellor often napped in a leather swivel chair near Godwin's desk. When someone called Godwin looking for Falwell, he'd wave them off. "Tell 'em I'm not here," he'd say, falling back asleep.

7. Immaculate Inflection

O N a Saturday afternoon in a classroom at West Point, the
elite military academy overlooking New York's Hudson
River, Chase McCool, a twenty-two-year-old senior at
Liberty, is on a verbal rampage. His opponents are two young men
with crew cuts and garbed in black dress uniforms, the lapels of
which are festooned with gold ship's anchors. They are students
from the U.S. Naval Academy.

McCool, wearing a blue striped shirt and peach tie, is bobbing
his head and stomping his foot on the floor as he sputters forth like
a verbal Gatling gun. He is not having a seizure. McCool is firing a
counterattack in a round of policy debate. At the precise moment
he ends, electronic beepers go off around the classroom. Now it's
time for the other team's "cross-x," an equally unintelligible blast
of verbiage attempting to take down McCool's arguments.

Policy debate is not remotely similar to the give-and-takes of presidential debates. It is evidence driven, formulaic, and technical. The more arguments you can squeeze into your allotted time the more points your opponent is forced to address. But the exchanges resemble what speed reading would sound like if it were audible— underwater. It is reminiscent of Pentecostals speaking in tongues. On his last cross-x, McCool averages nine words per second, or 540 words per minute.

McCool and his partner, Garrett Halydier, are members of Liberty's elite varsity squad. They are making the "affirmative" argument for military intervention in Iran. The debate consists of four constructive speeches, each followed by a cross-examination, then four rebuttals. The two teams will spend seventy-two minutes speaking and ten minutes preparing to speak. Prior to the tournament they will have spent days working on "evidence assignments" issued by their debate advisers, digging up bulletproof arguments to defend their fusillades of logic.

The tournament is in Thayer Hall, its gray stone walls conjuring the look of a medieval fortress. Dozens of college debate teams have assembled in matches spread across Thayer's entire fourth floor. In one hallway sit plastic barrels crammed with ice and Coke near bowls of potato chips, candy bars, pretzels, and stacks of boxed pizza. It has the feel of a typical college classroom building, except perhaps for the nearby video screens running simulated cruise-missile attacks.

Most universities in the debate circuit offer plaques and trophies as prizes—West Point is the only school to award its winner a weapon. It sits in a display case in the building's rotunda. The prize is a gold and silver cadet sword; it's surrounded by the military academy's parade hats. Novice and junior varsity winners are awarded the "tar buckets," as the hats are known. The winner of the varsity-level debate takes the saber home. Between rounds visiting team members crowd around the blade, ogling it like it were the sword Excalibur.

When the Naval Academy team arrives they barricade themselves on one side of their classroom behind a column of 10-gallon plastic tubs packed with files of research. Then they place a laptop on top of their plastic podium. Halydier chooses a less defensive position, setting up in the middle of the room a metal reading stand, the kind you see in an orchestra pit, and facing his audience. There are exactly three people in attendance: a middle-aged couple from Iowa— McCool's parents—and the tournament's judge, Heather Barnes.

Petite and amber-haired, Barnes is the former debate coach for a team Liberty has long feared: the University of Mary Washington. Its string of championship seasons rival Liberty's. It doesn't help that Barnes is an atheist who does not believe in Christian education. "You couldn't pay me to attend a Christian college," she says. As she watches the debate unfold, Barnes is impossible to read. She takes indecipherable notes on the right-hand columns of her scoring sheets, ranking the effectiveness of combatants' verbal thrusts and parries.

The number-two man on the navy team seems to falter on the second round. His face is flushed as he leans awkwardly into his laptop screen, draping his right leg behind his left as if in a frozen curtsey. Twice he is prompted by his partner to cut his counterpoints short. At the end of the round, he realizes he failed to defend himself against one of McCool's final attacks. "Dammit," he says under his breath.

Barnes stares at the naval team, as if to say, "Boy, that was stupid." As she waits for Halydier to respond, she contemplates her next move in a hand of freestyle solitaire on her laptop, which she plays between debate rounds. Halydier begins his counterpoint at muzzle velocity, hitting 460 words per minute. His delivery seems flawless; Halydier finishes by running down a list of biohazards renegade nations like Iran can obtain if they are not thwarted.

The debate over, Barnes prepares to render judgment. A few minutes of painful silence go by, then she clears her throat. "Alright." She turns to the navy team, launching a verbal fusillade of her own. "You totally sucked on the steel DA. You had some of the worst externals I've ever heard," she says. The "steel DA" was Navy's argument that Liberty's plan to stop weapons proliferation would disadvantage the U.S. steel industry. The "externals" were the chain of events they predicted would happen as a result of the Liberty plan. The navy team contended that oil prices keep Middle East economies thriving, allowing them to buy steel. A military strike, which McCool suggested, would be bad for U.S. hegemony because an economic hit to Middle East economies would diminish sales of U.S. military wares, thereby hurting the U.S. economy.

Barnes criticized Navy team's "cards," the term for research documents, and said they had left some of Liberty's points entirely unaddressed. "You can't let 'em get away with that. That was ridiculous." She continues to dress down the navy team, slamming them on point after point. When she is done, it's Liberty's turn.

Glaring at McCool and Halydier, she draws a long sigh. "You guys were seriously shallow on the line by line. You should have done a better job taking apart their impact terms. Your counter on steel sucked," she said, drumming her unpolished nails on the table. "Your arguments on steel were not strategic. Plus, you made the claim without the warrant. I was like, WTF?" McCool's eyes bugged out as he stared into space. Halydier looked down at the screen of his laptop. Barnes seemed disgusted by both teams. Even so, she would have to choose. "I'm going to give it to the aff," she says. The "aff" was Liberty's affirmative position. Liberty had won.

That day's competition would culminate in the "Partial Double Octafinal Round," followed by a final burst of elimination trials the next day. At the end of the three-day tournament Liberty would not win the sword or a tar bucket, but with a little help from an athiest, Liberty gained a respectable ranking.

The Falwells spend $14 million annually on Liberty's football squad and its eighteen NCAA-level sports teams. The debate team—its unofficial, nineteenth athletic program—costs a mere $500,000 a year. It's probably the best return on capital Falwell ever invested. The debate program has brought Liberty glory in both the secular and religious press. The team has ranked first in the nation for two years in a row, 2006–07, beating out Harvard, Princeton, and Yale, and bringing it heaps of praise from its peers.

Debate-team members are like the Jedis of Liberty; elite warriors who are seldom seen but constantly talked about. They are semicelebrities, allowed to miss (but must make up) tests if they happen to be on the road, which is often. Team members are required to maintain a 3.0 GPA. They embark on 1,000-mile bus trips, double up in Holiday Inns, work until the late hours of the night, and come back to face finals in other classes.

Falwell was never shy in describing the purpose of his debaters. It is to open another front in the war on secular culture with ground troops who are articulate and verbally superior. Its graduates, he believed, would win arguments and deliver the Christian world view in city, state, and federal courthouses. Some 75 percent of debate team grads have become lawyers. Ultimately, hoped Falwell, many will go on to become strict constructionist judges who are opposed to gay marriage and advocate rights for the unborn.

So far the biggest impact member of the team is its director, Brett O'Donnell, who took a leave of absence to become George W. Bush Jr.'s speech coach during the 2004 presidential campaign. O'Donnell left again to work full-time for Sen. John McCain's presidential run in 2007. It's the kind of buzz that attracted Stephanie Dillard, twenty, a sophomore on the debate squad. But for Dillard the campus's Christian identity was the real draw. "I don't want to be at a college where I have to compromise my morals or where my faith is constantly tested. If I went to a secular school I'm sure I'd be ridiculed and persecuted for my beliefs. As Christians we're supposed to let people know why we love Jesus, how Jesus can bring you salvation. Keeping quiet defeats the whole purpose of being Christian."

The 2007 incoming class of novices arrived on campus in mid-August, a month earlier than the rest of the campus, to get a jump on the intense schedule awaiting them. The debate program is structured like a pyramid. Novices are on the bottom, junior varsity in the middle, and varsity at the top. It can take four years to become a varsity member, a road littered with steep attrition. Typically only six students reach the pinnacle.

The year's incoming class began their debate camp in a small auditorium inside DeMoss Hall. Forty kids from a dozen states were there; half were men, half were women, and most were white. They had worked at bagel shops, law firms, candy factories, and Chick-fil-As. They were lifeguards, face painters, and amateur skydivers. A twenty-year-old Asian woman had just finished her fourth novel; a nineteen-year old from Tennessee explained his hobby was "cow-tipping" in the middle of the night. An eighteen-year-old had studied Navajo code talkers. "As iron sharpens iron, so one man sharpens another," read the back of one young man's T-shirt.

With O'Donnell on leave, the program is in the hands of a husband-and-wife team, Michael Hall and wife Heather, an attractive couple in their thirties who promise students: "This year you'll know more about the Middle East than anyone, except maybe a PhD."

At the class's first debate camp, Heather pushed her novices hard. Sitting at the front of the class, the slender Hall sat in a high chair, dressed casually in fuchsia waders, flip-flops, and a white T-shirt. With delicate cheekbones framed by tortoise-shell glasses and auburn hair pulled in a loose bun, she could easily be mistaken for a student. But there was nothing delicate about the complicated structures of logic and persuasion she was explaining. They are designed to knock down your opponent and keep him from recovering.

An argument is a claim supported by a warrant, but everything a debater claims has to address "harms," explains Hall. "It's one of the six prima facie burdens you have in making your first affirmative argument," she said, rapidly tapping a flip-flop against her foot. She got up and walked to the chalkboard to list the six burdens. Significance . . . Harms . . . Inherency . . . Topicality . . . The plan . . . Solvency. "If you want to remember these, you can probably think up an acronym," she said with a mischievous smile. Following the order of Hall's own list would produce "SHITTS," of course.

Unlike Liberty's law school or seminary students, the debate team sometimes flirts with doctrinal subversion, but no one seems to mind. On the larger campus, just the suggestion of vulgarity can draw a reprimand. Back in his dorm room, McCool is used to seeing the little green slips of paper checking off violations. Upon arriving at his dorm room one afternoon, McCool sat down on his food-stained sofa and spotted four of the slips push-pinned into his ceiling. They carried a dreaded warning: "Your room has not met our cleanliness standard." It was left for him and his roommates, who had found them and affixed them in anonymous rebellion.

Reprimands are usually issued while students are in convocations they are required to attend on Mondays, Wednesdays, and Fridays. Before students leave they are supposed to perform what they call their "quad job"—vacuuming and making beds. "You have to earn tons of reprimands before they mean something, and even then, it's not a big deal," says McCool. After suffering the blistering critiques of debate judges, in which he was told he "sucked," getting berated by a residence assistant (RA) seemed minor by comparison. The RAs enforce a campus code of behavior modeled after the Bob Jones University's code of conduct, only Liberty's rules have been liberalized. The practice of witchcraft carries the same sanction as having an abortion ($500 fine plus eighteen reprimands).

Jerry Falwell was ubiquitous on the Liberty campus. It wasn't hard to spot a large black Denali SUV with Falwell behind the wheel, cell phone glued to his ear, as the truck barreled down University Boulevard. He'd gun the engine as students crossed in front of him as if he were about to mow them down. The SUV was equipped with a locomotive horn, which he'd blow against unsuspecting pedestrians who shuddered at the high-decibel blast.

Practically every dean and veteran faculty member had, at one time, been the butt of his practical jokes. It was a Falwell tradition: In the heyday of the Moral Majority, when Falwell flew 300,000 miles a year, visiting as many as forty-four state capitals, he broke the monotony of his constant air travel by setting off stink bombs or rolling firecrackers down the aisle during takeoff.

Even Falwell's own funeral director, Paul Whitten, was not immune. Just a few days after Falwell's death, Whitten stood over Falwell's future gravesite on the lawn of the Carter Glass Mansion, recounting the last time he fell for a Falwell ruse. At another funeral the two had recently attended together, Falwell motioned for Whitten to come see him. As soon as he got within arm's reach, Falwell sucker-punched him in the solar plexus. "I keeled over. It was a real punch," says Whitten, wincing at the memory. "Jerry laughed 'til he was red in the face."

Falwell also found amusement listening to the horror stories students related in coming to campus, or trying to, for the first time. The first thing freshmen encounter on their way to Liberty is Lynchburg's highway system, the most confusing set of roads in Virginia. Approaching Liberty's campus from downtown Lynchburg, drivers literally finds themselves heading north on 29, east on 460, and south on 501—all at the same time. Even students using GPS have gotten lost. The campus sits on the lower slopes of Candler's Mountain. The only easy thoroughfare to navigate, Route 29—Wards Road—runs along Liberty's western border. A once sleepy stretch of farmland, it has sprouted a string of student-friendly big-box retailers like Cracker Barrel, Barnes & Noble, Best Buy, and Wal-Mart. Most of these stores sit on land once owned by Jerry Jr.

The ring of highways around Liberty is good for retailers because they bring both local folks to their stores and shoppers from outlying areas like Bedford County. The roads extend their market beyond Lynchburg's 64,000 residents to the larger population area of 240,000. What is access for shoppers with cars, however, is a barrier to students on foot. Unlike, say, the University of Virginia, Liberty's campus is not integrated into a neighborhood filled with stores and restaurants.

The school's eastern boundary is Route 460, on the opposite side of campus from Wards Road. Alongside 460 a new line of dorms is marching up the side of the mountain. To get to campus from these rooms, students either have to drive, hitchhike, or descend through a $400,000 pedestrian tunnel Jerry Jr. has drilled below the highway for students to get to campus without dodging cars moving at freeway speed. To get to the big-box stores along the Wards Road side of campus, students either have to drive (assuming one has a car; most students don't) or, more commonly, bushwhack their way down the mountain, vaulting over railroad tracks on their way to Wards Road. There, in order to avoid a half-mile walk to the nearest light, they must wait for a break in the traffic and dart across. Barnes & Noble is just across the highway from campus, but only a trickle of Liberty students shop there because few want to drive— it would mean losing their coveted parking spot on campus.

Liberty has grown along the side of a mountain, but much of its land is treeless. Its sixty buildings are spread over a two-mile clearing, running from the circular Vines Center arena at one end to the red-brick entrance of Thomas Road church at the other. The giant, preexisting Ericsson Building sets up a clash between newly created colonial facades and the severe, rectilinear roof lines of a former manufacturing plant. It's big box meets Jefferson.

Liberty is unusually large for a fundamentalist school, but more unique for the fact that it is a university attached to a church and the Liberty Channel television network. Some of Liberty's faculty host their own shows on the channel. Professor Ed Hindson hosts a program, *It's Later Than You Think,* devoted to studying the end of the world.

The portly, bespectacled Hindson is dean of the Institute for Biblical Studies, part of Liberty's School of Religion. He has five degrees and has lectured on religion at Oxford and Harvard. He is best known for his study of the Rapture, the prediction in the Book of Revelation that Christ will return to earth and take those who have converted to Christianity with him. Among his books: *Antichrist Rising, Approaching Armegeddon* and *Is the Antichrist Alive Today?* He has also collaborated with *Left Behind* series author Tim LaHaye, coauthor of a series of prophetic novels about a group of people abandoned after the Rapture. Having sold 65 million copies, the success of the novels prompted LaHaye to start an academic component to his book and put Hindson in charge of it. The eighty-three-year-old LaHaye was a founding board member of the Moral Majority. When the organization folded LaHaye turned his attention to Liberty, pouring $3.5 million into a student center, an ice rink, and the Institute for Biblical Studies at the School of Religion. The institute is essentially Hindson and his television show. It is not for the theological faint-of-heart.

On one episode in 2007, Hindson blasted Islam as a "false religion" advanced by a "false prophet." A video screen behind him explodes in images of mushroom clouds as he warns that Islamic fanatics are planning a "Muslim millennium," wherein they will convert the entire world to Islam. A photo of Iran's president Ahmadinejad suddenly appears, backlit by a wall of flame. Hindson explains that the Rapture will be signaled by the coming of "trumpet judgements"—environmental catastrophes, mainly—which will lead to the "destruction of planet earth itself." A message crawls along the bottom of the screen, as if this were a telethon: "Jesus could come at any time!" When Jesus does come, he says, "The people of Israel will be converted to the true messiah."

Hindson caps off his prophecies with a message strangely incongruous to the mayhem of the rest of the show. "The only hope for peace in the future is when people come to know the prince of peace," he says.

There are no Islamists on Liberty's faculty, but there is Ergun Mehmet Caner, a former Sunni muslim who converted to fundamentalism and is now president of the Liberty Theological Seminary. If there's anyone on campus who is heir to Falwell's charisma, it's Caner. Bald, bearded, and beefy, Caner grew up in Turkey, emigrated, and converted to Christianity in 1982. After he was disowned by his family he earned a masters of divinity from Southeastern Baptist Theological Seminary at Wake Forest in North Carolina. His 2002 book, *Unveiling Islam,* was a best-seller. Caner says, "America isn't homogenous anymore," he told the *News & Advance*'s Ron Brown. "We look like a bowl of Fruity Pebbles. Like me, many people have olive skin. We can't understand them unless we understand their culture."[1]

As dean of the seminary, the forty-two-year-old Caner teaches Theology 678, a course on sects and cults. After he converted he says he realized that "Jesus strapped himself to a cross so that I wouldn't have to strap myself to a bomb." He is still devoted to the faith of his childhood, but now sees it through a fundamentalist Christian lens. His theology course is unique for the way it opens a window on other faiths. He invites their adherents to come and discuss their spirituality in the form of a public interview, C-SPAN-style.

What students learn in this course comes directly from practitioners of competing religions. Caner is a rigorous interviewer, bringing in Mormons, Baha'is, and others. His questions are provocative, but they usually don't provoke his guests. He does not attempt to entrap or convert, simply to hit his subjects with his best shot, and learn from their defense.

One such guest was pastor Mel White, a man who had ghostwritten Falwell's own autobiography in 1987. White had since had a spectacular falling out with Falwell when White, four years after the book came out, announced he was gay. White and his partner moved into an apartment across the street from Thomas Road Baptist Church and began attending church on Sunday mornings. Anytime Falwell said anything negative about gays, White would stand and hang his head in silent protest.

It was a strange twist for White, a man who had a successful career ghostwriting for some of the giants of conservative Christianity: W. A. Criswell, Billy Graham, Pat Robertson, and Jim Bakker. Keeping himself in the closet turned out to be a losing battle. During his twenty-two-year marriage, he tried to "cure" his homosexuality with electroshock treatment, psychotherapy, fasting, and a Catholic exorcism. Nothing worked. He tried to commit suicide, but botched it, and wound up in a hospital instead.

White started an activist group for gay clergy called Soulforce and is described by locals as the "the best-known Sodomite in Lynchburg." He took the opportunity during his interview with Caner to correct that label. He pointed out that the Sodomites of the Bible were people who closed the gates of Sodom to the poor and sick. That piqued God's anger. "I may be queer, but I'm no Sodomite," quipped White.

Caner's session with White was a milestone for White, and for Liberty: It was the first time White was allowed on campus for most of 2006, after his organization, Soulforce, sent twenty of its activists to illegally trespass on campus as a protest against Liberty's position that homosexuality is a sin. They were arrested. White and Caner debated polygamy and bisexuality; why Solomon had one thousand wives and whether God really loves everyone, including gays. White jousted with Caner and tried to disarm his audience with jokes. Mentioning the Rapture, he said: "What if it's already happened and God decided he didn't want any of us?"

White took issue with the fundamentalist mission, criticizing the notion that he, as a Christian, should have to advance his faith by "cornering, convincing and converting" people. White recalled a statement by Billy Graham, whom he said was once asked, " 'Who goes to heaven and who goes to hell?' " Graham reportedly responded, "Thank God that that's God's business, not mine."

White criticized the mingling of theology with the political process, saying the Bible sanctioned no such behavior. Then Caner asked White: "What is the difference between Martin Luther King imposing his faith and applying it to politics, and Jerry Falwell taking his faith and applying it to politics?" White said that Jesus' agenda was to pursue "justice, mercy, and truth," which is identical to King's mission. The agenda of fundamentalist Christians, by contrast, could be seen by their support by a recent move by the state of Virginia to ban any form of civil union among gays. "They want to kick us out of Virginia and banish us from the state," he said. "They are the Sodomites, not us."

White distributed pamphlets to students describing what the Bible doesn't say about homosexuality; students quoted Scripture back to White, telling him what it does. It was a polite exchange until White caught a student in the audience smirking. Suddenly he welled up with rage, raising his voice. "Your teachings are killing my sisters and brothers," said White. "Your words against us are not benign. They have tragic consequences." White came prepared with evidence. He read a selection of some of the most venom-filled direct-mail solicitations Falwell had produced against gays. According to one mailing:

> Homosexuality is perverse. They're demanding a sewer of moral filth; a place of spiritual anarchy; an environment that is incredibly dangerous to our children; a culture that despises the Christian faith and morality. Mark my words: the primary target of the homosexual is the nation's public schools and our impressionable children. They have set out to destroy the meaning of family in America, to rewrite the definition of what we hold dear and sacred.

Every Wednesday convocation at 6 P.M., Caner hosts a one-man show called, *Games Christians Play*. The 6,000-seat Thomas Road sanctuary is usually packed for this event down to every last seat. The show opens with a performance from a Christian rock band, with multicolored stage lights shining like lasers across the darkened hall. Caner is like a spiritual rock star to his students; a fearless yet vulnerable sage. He's a natural showman: one moment raving at the delusions he says Christians have when they think they can cut deals with God; the next moment he has calmed down, speaking in a whisper, his voice seeping with emotion.

He keeps his faculty entertained with a blog of his musings on campus life. In one posting he tells his fellow profs that the rules of working at a fundamentalist university may seem rigorous, but that life at Liberty is bliss compared to the rules governing independent U.S. schools in 1872. He posted the nineteenth-century rules for his fellow professors to review:

1. Teachers each day will fill lamps, clean chimneys.

2. Each teacher will bring a bucket of water and a scuttle of coal for the day's session.

3. Make your pens carefully. You may whittle nibs to the individual taste of the pupils.

4. Male teachers may take one evening each week for courting purposes, or two evenings a week, if they go to church regularly.

5. After ten hours in school, the teachers may spend the remaining time reading the Bible or other good books.

6. Women teachers who marry or engage in unseemly conduct will be dismissed.

7. Every teacher should lay aside from each pay a goodly
   sum of his earnings for his benefit during his declining
   years so that he will not become a burden on society.

8. Any teacher who smokes, uses liquor in any form, fre-
   quents pool or public halls, or gets shaved in a barbershop
   will give good reason to suspect his worth, intention, integrity, and honesty.

9. The teacher who performs his labor faithfully and without fault for five years will be given an increase of
   twenty-five cents per week in his pay, providing the
   board of education approves.

Falwell hired Caner, in part, because of his love of religious history. It inspired Falwell's passion for his own historical obsessions,
which included the building of the University of Notre Dame. For
much of his life Notre Dame was Jerry Falwell's personal para-
digm. It's an inspiring story: the school that produced Knute
Rockne, Joe Montana, and Raghib "The Rocket" Ismail was begun
in the middle of the nineteenth century by French missionaries
who spoke no English. It grew from a log-cabin chapel, expanding
into a full-fledged university recognized by the state of Indiana in
1844. Even then, "Notre Dame was just a few buildings with
swampy ground surrounded by henhouses, outhouses, pigsties, and
cow sheds. At best the food was bad and the water worse."[2]

Its law school opened in 1869; an engineering progam in 1873.
After the entire school burnt to the ground, its founder, Rev. Edward Frederick Sorin, rebuilt the campus even bigger than its prior

size. Like Falwell, Sorin created Notre Dame in the image of his own outsized ambitions. Like Liberty, Notre Dame was always short on money, especially in the early days, according to Notre Dame biographers Jim Langford and Jeremy Langford. As they write: "Notre Dame worked diligently not to turn students away—allowing some to pay their way through manual labor, livestock or long-term loans."[3] Father Sorin used his own inheritance to finance the school and convinced others to do the same. He solicited "funds from the Societies of the Propagation of the Faith in Lyon and Paris, begging throughout the east and Northeast and other areas around the country where Catholics congregate, and signing promissary notes on his own authority and then mailing the bills back to France for his order to pay. He even sent a band of Brothers out west during the Gold Rush of 1849–50. Not only did the Brothers return empty-handed, one of their own died on the trip."[4]

Falwell had Epsilon and Art Williams to help him grow and put his financial house in order. Notre Dame had the "Burns Legacy" and Rev. Theodore M. Hesburgh. Father James Aloysius Burns was the school's tenth president.

> He fought for the establishment of an investment board that included laymen, then convinced his religious colleagues to turn over to the new board, heavy with experienced businessmen, the control and administration of University funds . . . The Rockefeller and Carnegie Foundations liked his message and offered $250,000 and $75,000 respectively—if he could raise an additional

$750,000. He did. That million-plus was Notre Dame's first endowment, . . .[5]

Hesburgh, Notre Dame's 15th president, spanning the years 1952 to 1987, transformed the university. Over those years Notre Dame's operating budget grew from $10 million to $177 million, and its endowment from $9 million to $350 million. Enrollment leaped from 5,000 to 9,600; its faculty doubled to 950. Hesburgh held fifteen presidential appointments and 150 honorary degrees— the most ever awarded to an American—and the Medal of Freedom, the nation's highest civilian honor.

Today, Notre Dame is regularly among the top twenty of *U.S. News*'s national university rankings. Its grads include astronauts and federal judges. In 2005, nearly thirty of its grads had become presidents of colleges and universities. Its endowment now exceeds $2.4 billion.

These academic and financial achievements get overlooked by Notre Dame's greatness on the gridiron. What first made a little college in Indiana a household name was the brilliance of a famous football coach. Knute Rockne's record was 105 wins, 12 losses, and 5 ties before he died in the prime of his career in a plane crash in 1931.

As the football crowds grew to 50,000 per game, Notre Dame's star ascended . . . In 1920, for example, the school's 67-member faculty taught 1,207 who paid tuition, room, and board of about $574 per year. During the next decade, while the Fighting Irish football team won national prominence for the University, Notre

Dame's faculty would increase and its enrollment would nearly triple—to 3,227 in 1930–31.[6]

Until recently, Falwell's own football team found no such glory. That was bitterly disappointing to Falwell, whose favorite sport was football. He had been captain of his high school football team. In 2005 the Liberty Flames ended their season with a 1–10 record. That season the team sold a total of 135 season tickets. Falwell fired the coach, Ken Karcher, and replaced him with Danny Rocco, a former special teams coach for the New York Jets who'd spent five seasons as an assistant coach with the University of Virginia. Rocco had big game experience: He appeared in three bowl games as a player and another ten as a coach.

Falwell may have found his own Knute Rockne in Rocco. In his first season Rocco took the Flames to 6–5 and broke twelve different team records. The Flames clinched three kickoff-return touchdowns, something no other college team in the U.S. managed that year. In 2007 Liberty went 8–3 and won the Big South conference championship. The team sold 2,000 season tickets in 2007 and tripled its average attendance to 14,000. Rocco can't thank Falwell's church for divine favor—he doesn't attend Thomas Road, but a nondenominational church in Bedford county. That made no difference to Falwell, who knew winning meant everything.

Besides football, Falwell admired Notre Dame's religiosity. It is no less intense than Liberty's. The school has a chapel in each of its residence halls—each week sixty-eight masses are held in dorms. What Falwell could never fathom was the school's welcoming attitude toward its gay students. There is a standing committee at Notre Dame of students and faculty who meet regularly to monitor the needs of "gay, lesbian, bisexual, and questioning students on the Notre Dame campus." The university hosts a reception for first-year gay students in the fall, weekly socials at its student center, and an annual retreat for gay students. The Campus Ministry hosts Solidarity Sunday each fall, in which students pray together for a clearer understanding of sexual identities and an end to anti-gay violence. The ministry also maintains a library in which monographs and books related to gay issues are stockpiled. In 1999, Notre Dame embraced another inclusive milestone—this one involving its school mascot. For the first time, Notre Dame had an African American leprechaun.

Another Liberty faculty member with a different slant on history is Marcus Ross, an assistant professor of biology who teaches a mandatory course called History of Life. The thirty-year-old Ross, resembling a young Dennis Miller, drives a red scooter to campus. He is younger than many of his students. Ross graduated with a doctoral degree in geosciences from the University of Rhode Island, where his thesis focused on mosasaurs, a class of marine lizards, which, as he asserted in his dissertation, disappeared 65 million years ago at the close of the Cretaceous period.

Of course, Ross teaches nothing of the sort at Liberty. His course is based on the concept that God created all viruses, bacteria, fungi, protozoans, and every species on earth over a six-day period in 4004 BC. Ross does not believe dinosaurs lived 65 million years ago, but coexisted with man until 2300 BC, when a flood destroyed them. He believes, as the Old Testament chronicles, that Adam lived to an age of 930 years, and that Methuselah died at age 969. With the Bible as his preeminent scientific source, he teaches that human life spans began to diminish after the "fall" of man.

One of Liberty's key microbiology textbooks, *The Genesis of Germs,* explains why:

> A creation-science viewpoint predicts that all living organisms were originally good and the human body likely had a symbiotic relationship with microbes. A remnant of the pre-Fall environment, which was free of disease, suggests the immune system was originally designed to interact positively with microbes. After corruption and the Curse, the immune system's interaction with microbes had to change, and now it has become a defensive body system, screening for dangerous pathogens and toxins.[7]

The textbook's Chapter 10 opens with a black-and-white illustration of a robed skeleton holding a scythe atop a grunting, scraggly-haired stallion. The introductory passage sounds more appropriate for Ed Hindson's school of prophecy than a biology textbook. According to the text:

> It will get worse before it gets better. There is little doubt that the fourth horseman, pestilence, has saddled up and is charging at us with lance poised. However, we can parry his thrusts with obedience to the Creator and His Word. We read about horsemen (i.e. angels in Revelation) that will bring judgment and this will include plagues and pestilences that will wipe out a quarter of the population. We do not know what disease it may be. It could be influenza, smallpox, bubonic plague, SARS, ebola, measles. It could be a germ that mankind has never seen before. We

just do not know what pathogen it will be. We only know that it will be terrible. There is hope only for the believer.[8]

There aren't many schools who teach this brand of fundamentalist biology, also known as "young earth creationism." But Ross's course has changed minds. A recent survey of his students found big jumps in the number of those who at the beginning of the course did not believe the earth is less than 10,000 years old or that dinosaurs and man coexisted, and those who did.

A few of Ross's critics aren't so much angry over what he teaches but what they call his dishonesty in pretending he believed in evolution and traditional geological science simply to earn his his PhD. Some of his colleagues want him to return his doctoral degree to Rhode Island University—one even suggested he be stoned to death with tribolytes. A "kerfuffle" is how Ross describes the controversy. Earning a PhD does not mean believing in everything it stands for, he says.

Geology students at other universities have it in for Ross, too. Evelyn Martinique Mervine, a graduate student in geology at the MIT/Woods Hole Oceanographic Institute, brought dozens of responses (almost all in support) from a pithy post in a geology blog:

In my free time, I try to date men, but mostly I'm dating rocks these days. More formally, I am a graduate student in training to become an argon-argon isotope geochronologist. Basically, I am learning how to use argon isotopes to determine dates for rocks . . . this spring I am working on obtaining ten dates from a group of volcanic rocks from the Ninetyeast Ridge, a 5000-km long hotspot track on in the Indian Ocean. I anticipate that my samples will range in age from about 40 million to 80 million years old. These ten age dates are going to require a solid three months of my time. This past week has been particularly grueling as we are trying to prepare a group of samples to send off to the nuclear reactor we use to turn potassium into argon, an important step in the argon-argon dating process. . . . Theoretically, someone with a Ph.D. in geology appreciates how difficult these dates are to obtain and understands the science behind the isotopic dating systems. I am angry because here is someone (Marcus Ross) who has good geological credentials . . . and he's essentially trying to discredit what is swiftly becoming my life's work . . . Having a Ph.D. geologist tell me that Earth is only 6,000 years old is absurd and makes me very angry and also very, very sad.[9]

Ross is unmoved. "It's incredible that people feel personally attacked by my mere existence."

ONE thing a conservative Christian student learns at Liberty, whether it's Bible studies or biology, is the articulate defense of fundamentalist doctrine. Second only to the debate program in teaching those skills is another boot camp for verbal jousting—this one on the other side of campus: Liberty's school of law. In commercials on the Liberty Channel, Dean Mat Staver says exactly what he thinks about the program: "The only school of law in the country worth attending." The view is not yet shared by the roughly 50 percent of debate graduates who went on to law school, in 2007 none of whom went to Liberty. Jerry Jr. might disagree with Staver's assessment, too (his alma mater is the law school at the University of Virginia).

In 2008 Chase McCool plans to break the mold. He is the first debate team member to apply to Liberty's law school. He plans to do his honors thesis on the political implications of the overturning of *Roe v. Wade* on the Republican Party. "The abortion issue is good for us because it holds the party together. But if that's gone, what do we focus on? What's our next big schtick?" he asks.

Of the 187 law schools in the United States accredited by the American Bar Association (ABA), 54 are affiliated with a religion. It is not easy to project judicial gravitas inside the confines of what was once a telecom factory, but Staver is trying. The long, wide hallways have been refaced with drywall, painted beige, and are sparsely furnished with red upholstered chairs, leather couches, and small, faux antique clocks. Turn a corner and you might suddenly run into a hallway with an almost monasterylike ambience. There are groupings of large scented candles on carved-wood pedestals. Next to overstuffed couches are small tables on which artificial ivy appears to grow out of jewelry boxes. So far, the school has cost Liberty $14 million. It is money spent to project an aura of refinement and that has not yet really arrived. What look like medieval tapestries outside Staver's office are really elegant fakes made in North Carolina.

The centerpiece of the law school is a room whose door posts a listing of the Ten Commandments. The 4,395-square-foot room is an exact replica of the U.S. Supreme Court, right down to its four columns, oak bench, and rake seating. It took a year and over one million dollars to build. It is one part teaching classroom, one part recruiting tool, and one part object of inspiration. In an introductory video shown to first-year law students, the flavor of the school's unvarnished mission is conveyed by Family Research Council President Tony Perkins, who says, "We can't defend Christianity without Christian lawyers and judges." Next comes Phyllis Schlafly, the conservative political activist who helped defeat the Equal Rights Amendment in the 1970s. "Secular groups are trying to change our society into something it never was and shouldn't be." Liberty's school of law is based on precisely the same brand of activist lawyering Mat Staver waged to repeal the Jefferson-era laws on church power.

At a "barristers orientation" for the class of 2010 in August 2006, Staver told the story of Liberty's battle to stay alive in the vernacular of Biblical narrative. Staver is a former Seventh-Day Adventist pastor turned lawyer who represented the Orlando Magic basketball team, Marriott, and Taco Bell before he and wife Anita established Liberty Counsel, a kind of conservative ACLU. His work for Liberty Counsel seems a perfect blend of waging religious war with the spirit of competitive sports. He started Liberty Counsel in 1989 by taking on a string of controversial cases. Staver first gained national attention when he threatened to sue a Jacksonville public library after it threw a Harry Potter party and handed out a "Hogwarts' Certificate of Accomplishment" to each of the two hundred kids who attended. Some parents complained the library was distributing "witchcraft certificates." Staver said that since witchcraft is a religion, handing out the certificates was a violation of the First Amendment's establishment clause. The library agreed not to hold such events in the future.

Since 1989, says Staver, Liberty Counsel has won 86 percent of the cases it has taken on. During an average year, Liberty Counsel is involved in eighty cases and its staff members appear in 1,300 print, radio, and television interviews. Its Web site receives 120,000 unique visitors a month. Liberty Counsel meets monthly in Washington with other groups to advance passage of marriage amendments to state constitutions, even drafting some of them. One was the Florida Marriage Protection Amendment, which the ACLU tried to block from appearing on the ballot. The Florida Supreme Court ruled 7-0 in Staver's favor.

He successfully defended a Christian family who runs a bed-and-breakfast against a complaint filed by a lesbian couple who wanted to use the inn to hold a gay civil marriage ceremony. He defended a Christian businessman who refused to duplicate a pro-gay videotape submitted to him by lesbian activists. He has a handful of victories under his belt in enacting parental notification laws regarding abortions.

Staver's group came to the aid of a Baldwinsville, New York, kindergartner, Antonio Peck, whose parents contended his school artwork was censored by his teacher for its religious content. The assignment, which Peck completed in the summer of 1999, was to create a poster on the environment. In the center of Peck's illustration was a church; on the left side of the page was a cut-out drawing of Jesus in a flowing robe, kneeling in prayer. Peck's drawing was posted with the rest of his classmates' on a cafeteria wall, but was deemed "too religious" by his teachers, so the left side of the page was folded back to make Jesus disappear. School officials contended the work violated the separation of church and state, and were apparently afraid parents would assume religion was being taught in class.

Staver sued to get a precedent established that no public school in the United States can censor the religious viewpoints of students in response to an assignment. A three-judge panel on the Second U.S. Circuit Court of Appeals, who then included Judge Samuel Alito, ruled unanimously in Staver's favor. The U.S. Supreme Court later let the ruling stand.

Juxtapositions tell much of what the law school wants to convey. There is a portrait of the prophet Jeremiah near the Magna Carta. The Ten Commandments are displayed near the U.S. Constitution. Along the hallway leading to the Supreme Court classroom hangs a line of framed portraits of U.S. presidents alongside a quote from each asserting the primacy of God to the governance of the nation. John Adams is quoted thus:

> Suppose a nation in some distant region should take the Bible for their only law book and every member should regulate his conduct by the precepts there exhibited! Every member would be obliged in conscience to temperance, frugality and industry; to justice, kindness and charity to his fellow men, and to piety, love and reverence toward almighty God . . . what a utopia, what a paradise would this region be.

Near the center of the school is its 250,000-title collection Ehrhorn Library, stored in bound volumes and on microfiche. There are classic works by Friedrich Nietzsche and Søren Kierkegaard, alongside contemporary books on religion like *The Jesus Machine* by *U.S. News* writer Dan Gilgoff, a not-so-flattering look at Religious Right leader James Dobson. But there is little doubt this is

Jerry Falwell's law library. The collection carries thirty works on George Washington; twenty-two books about Ronald Reagan. Sections on divorce, prostitution, and abortion are grouped together. There are twenty-eight books on homosexuality and gay rights; one hundred and fourteen books on abortion.

The purpose of being a law student at Liberty, as described to them by their chaplain, is profoundly simple. "Your duty is to believe," he said. But they also have some unique responsibilities. There can be no acts of subversion, no bending of the rules, because law school students are expected to adhere to even stricter standards than the campus at large. The class of 2010 got a taste of these expectations when they were paid a visit during orientation week by director of student affairs Dorothy Nijakowski. She began the session with a prayer: "Heavenly Father, I've been thanking you for the privilege of working with these students. Sometimes I think I'm not worthy, I'm not capable. But you remind me that I'm dependent on you," she said. "Help me Lord in being articulate, in being understandable."

Then Nijakowski laid down the law. "Rule number one: the absolute goal of everything we do at the law school is to bring glory to God. That includes our reputation," she said. "Every policy, rule, and code is based on Scripture. Therefore we will not back down on them. Next summer you're going to begin internships. You're going to need a letter of recommendation from faculty. They're going to base it on a perception of you as a Christian."

At West Point, cheating results in expulsion. At Liberty it draws a reprimand. What really sets the alarm bells off at Liberty's law school is personal conduct. "Think about things that would make people question your integrity," says Nijakowski. "Take voice-mail messages. I'd recommend you not do silly ones. You're in law school, make it professional. Also, anything off color. Scripture says, 'Do not let any unwholesome talk come out of your mouth.' People talk, and if they think you're not living a Christian life, they tend to let us know."

She continued, "People are watching you. They're watching you as a Christian, they're watching you as a law student. Believe me, if they have a chance to make fun of you, they'll do it. An off-color voice-mail message is an infraction." The same goes for Facebook and MySpace pages, she said. Posting "off-color" messages will draw an infraction because to do so undermines Liberty's mission.

Nijakowski finished her carrot-and-stick admonitions with a practical offer. "If a car is seen outside of a girl or boyfriend's house, that's an infraction of the law school's honor code. Cohabitating is definitely an infraction," she said. "If you're currently living with a boy or girlfriend, I've been given approval to give you three weeks to make other arrangements, to find you roommates. We're not trying to trip you up. Come to me and tell me about it, and it will go nowhere beyond our conversation. We hope you want to follow these rules because it's God's plan. But even if you don't, at least abide by them because they're the rules we live by here, and you'll need a recommendation for your internships.

8. LORDS OF LYNCHBURG

IGH atop the southern face of Candler's Mountain, just two miles from the Liberty law school, is the site of Jerry Falwell's last dream. Called Liberty Village, it was a venture some likened to a Christian utopia. Its streets are named after Falwell family members and friends. There is Macel Circle, Jonathan Lane, and Westover Place, the latter named for Falwell's longtime aide, Duke Westover. But on a humid August afternoon in 2007, these streets were deserted. The only humans in sight were five men in black wearing flak jackets and toting rifles. They were members of the Lynchburg police department's tactical weapons unit. Creating a ghost town for the local SWAT team to stage maneuvers wasn't exactly what Falwell had in mind when he conceived the project.

Liberty Village (LV) was a final step in Falwell's cradle-to-grave vision. On 140 acres of mountaintop land was to be a master-planned luxury retirement development. Its marketing team promoted LV as a "private country club community that offers all the amenities of a world class resort." It would be anchored by a 1,135-unit apartment complex consisting of villas, carriage homes, townhouses, and condominiums. As always, Falwell thought big. The development would include a clubhouse, a movie theater, a supermarket, a village green, and a chapel. A brochure promised a faith-based lifestyle: "The spiritual heart of our community is the intimate Chapel, with its soaring steeple, inspiring you to spiritual relaxation and meditation." Other amenities LV would offer were a computer center, three restaurants, and a swimming pool. There would be boccie and shuffleboard, tennis courts, and a playground for grandchildren. Its promoters said Liberty Village would have its own social director who would organize golf banquets, even though LV was only big enough to support a putting green.

Falwell hired a development partner who broke ground on the project in 2001. The next year Falwell posed with a scale model of Liberty Village, spread out in lilliputian detail on a display stand the size of a pool table. It may have been grandiose, but Liberty Village was by no means a bad idea. By 2001, Liberty University had become Lynchburg's second largest employer, after with a faculty of 800 and a staff of 2,000. When they reached retirement age might they not be persuaded to live out their golden years at the top of a mountain in a Christ-friendly environment? Lynchburg itself has been becoming a retirement destination in its own right. Falwell thought he had struck the right deal with New York–based Savoy Senior Housing. It was run by Jacob Frydman, a brash young Manhattan entrepreneur who had just made a failed bid to buy the construction company that built the Empire State Building.

Falwell formed a limited partnership with Frydman to build LV on land owned by TRBC Ministries, the predecessor to Jerry Falwell Ministries. Falwell sold the land for $600,000 to the partnership. Falwell's ministries would annually receive 2.5 percent of the price of every home sold or 10 percent of the net profits, whichever was higher. Frydman obtained a $20-million loan from a bank in South Boston, Virginia, to begin construction.

Falwell promoted Liberty Village on the *Gospel Hour,* generating what he said were two hundred leads a week on prospective buyers from Richmond to Roanoke. But the partnership failed to capitalize on the leads and soon began running short on money, says Jerry Jr. Contractors began filing some $3 million in mechanics liens and lawsuits against Savoy. Falwell stopped marketing LV altogether on the *Gospel Hour* in early 2003. Frydman soon filed for bankruptcy protection. The property sat in disrepair for the next three years, until Jerry Jr. found a new developer who would turn the venture into a modest life care facility. Its new developer couldn't raise the capital needed to buy the property out of bankruptcy, so Liberty bought back the land for a loss. Some of LV's handful of existing homes are now being used as housing for married couples enrolled at Liberty.

Real estate was the financial foundation of most of Falwell's ventures. Luckily, most of them turned out better than Liberty Village. Whenever Falwell backed an idea with the full force of his personality and vision, sooner or later it usually succeeded. Liberty Village failed because Falwell, like a classic entrepreneur, put all his energy into a vision, then let his attention to detail fade as as an out-of-state partner took over his dream.

As influential as he had been in national politics, meeting with heads of states and being consulted on future Supreme Court appointments, Falwell had surprisingly limited political clout in his own hometown of Lynchburg. He could help get presidents elected yet couldn't get his own candidate for local city council into office. He had little success dabbling in local political races. In the 1970s, he backed Chauncey Spencer's run for a local city council seat. Spencer had run liquor for Falwell's father in the 1930s. He left the city, went on to become a famous pioneer in black aviation, then returned to Lynchburg. Spencer ran as an outsider against an entrenched political machine. Falwell not only gave him his backing, he contributed $10,000 to his campaign. Spencer was soundly defeated.

Falwell had a political ally in Mayor Carl Hutcherson Jr., elected in 2000, until fallout from a financial transaction between the two ended the mayor's reign. In 2005, Hutcherson asked Falwell for a $32,500 donation to Trinity New Life Development Corporation, a community center run by Hutcherson that was part of a Methodist church he had founded. Some of the money would be used to pay rent Hutcherson was behind on for the community center, he told Falwell. When Hutcherson got the money he used it not to pay back rent, but his own back taxes.

An FBI investigator began looking into the payment. Hutcherson created a dummy board of directors and fabricated what he said were minutes from meetings of the board authorizing the money to be used as a personal loan to himself. In May 2006, a jury found Hutcherson guilty of seven felony counts, including mail and bank fraud, making false statements to an FBI agent, and obstructing justice. During the trial, it turned out that Hutcherson had also made himself payee on social security accounts belonging to two disabled members of his church. He used the money to buy a stereo system and to pay off his cable bill.

Falwell had a complicated relationship with the city of Lynchburg. Being tax exempt, his church and university make no direct contributions to the tax rolls. Yet the city must grudgingly accept that Lynchburg is Falwell country—one-third of Lynchburg's population belong to Thomas Road Baptist Church. Liberty's 10,700 students and 700 faculty bring a lot of business to Lynchburg. Not blue-chip retailers like Nieman Marcus or Sephora, but businesses that exist on land which was, not long ago, just alfalfa fields.

The church holds an annual "Super Conference" inside the Vines basketball arena where pastors and worship leaders come to debate the strategies of soul winning. The event brings about 3,000 visitors to Lynchburg, selling out hotels and packing local restaurants with those who come to hear Rick Warren and Franklin Graham, son of Billy Graham. Each week the church hosts a giant recruiting event, where 147 community groups meet and invite new members to attend. About 2,200 people show up for these meetings, running from guitar workshops and bass fishing to painting, quilting, and "gobbler" hunting.

The church's men's ministry, Gatekeepers, gets about 1,000 men and boys of hunting age to turn out for its annual Beast Feast. Attendees compete in shooting competitions and sit in on seminars where they might learn how to score the antlers of a buck or use a scope on a crossbow. Vendors show up in camoflauge suits, making them appear as if they'd been swallowed by a pile of leaves. Over a dinner of deer, alligator, bear, moose, and wild boar, attendees listen to hunting stories from Russell Thornberry, editor in chief of *Buckmasters,* the nation's largest whitetail hunting magazine.

Falwell hated hunting, but there were plenty of times he wanted to shoot certain members of the city council. He took personal offense when the council chose a "vision statement" in 2006 for Lynchburg which omitted the word "faith." Council member Mike Gillette argued against using the word at a council retreat, saying that it could be mistaken as "code" for Falwell's church. A few days later at a church sermon, Falwell counterattacked. "You're right, Mike, we're willing to accept that as a badge of honor. But I would suspect that there are one hundred or more pastors in Lynchburg who would not agree that faith belongs only to Thomas Road. There are so many great churches and a synagogue in this town. Faith belongs to any and all who believe, not just to Thomas Road Baptist Church. . . .

"Suppose Mike Gillette had said in the city council retreat the other day that we don't want Lynchburg to be known by its Jewish people or its Muslim people or its African American people. The newspapers would clobber him. But because he was able to say, 'We don't want Lynchburg to be known because of its evangelical Christians'—using faith as a code word for Evangelical Christians—no one says a blooming word. It's politically correct to slam Christians, but nobody else. Well, slam on and I'll just slam back." The city did not agree. It kept the word "faith" out of its statement.

Falwell had better luck the next month, when another controversy erupted around the three acres he and Jerry Jr. had cleared near the top of Candler's Mountain to construct a giant monogram with the letters "L-U." According to one plan, the center of the logo would have a gas-fired ignition system that would shoot a fountain of flame from between the letters every time the Liberty

Flames scored a touchdown. After Liberty erected two, 200-foot-long test letters made out of white plastic sheeting at the site, an editorial in the *News & Advance* denounced the Falwells' attempt at branding the mountain and ran a page of letters opposed to it. As one letter writer put it: "What has happened to Candler's Mountain is an abomination. Jerry Falwell has erased God's living creation, the work of his hand, and replaced it with Jerry's own logo."

Jerry Jr. fought back, penning a half-page op-ed in the *News & Advance* reminding readers of Liberty's strong environmental track record in its stewardship of the land, noting that mountain logos near universities are common. Besides, he wrote, "Letter writers should understand that Liberty has no obligations to preserve its lands as forests forever." The Falwells did make a few concessions to city planners; they reduced the size of the landscaping beds. The city allowed the Falwells to enact a permanent logo.

Like the state's other forty cities, Lynchburg is independent of the county around it. That means there is always competition for tax dollars between the two. Parcels of land donated to Falwell's ministries or purchased by them often spilled across city/county lines, causing Falwell to deal separately with two entities often competing with each other. Matters were made worse when Lynchburg annexed vast tracks of land in 1976, adding a large part of Liberty's property to its jurisdiction. Falwell's land use would now be governed by Lynchburg's planning commission and city council. "Dad grew up at a time when there was no zoning," says Jerry Jr. "He was never comfortable with the idea that local government could tell you what to do with your property. That bugged him to no end. He thought zoning laws were un-American."

For his school and church, Falwell bought, sold, and received as gifts thousands of acres of Lynchburg land over the years. His personal land holdings were modest. At the time of his death, he and Macel owned five parcels of land worth $1.3 million, plus an interest in a family trust. His net worth was perhaps $2 million.

There's not much remaining from Hezekiah Falwell's original parcel of 1,500 acres in Falwell family hands. After Jerry Jr., the next biggest landowner is Falwell's twin brother Gene, who still lives in the Falwell family home on Old Rustburg Road. Gene owns about ninety acres of land running from his home to a nearby highway. It includes the family graveyard, sitting on a hillside encircled by a black wrought-iron fence in the middle of one of Gene's cow pastures. Jerry Jr. incorporated the graveyard and registered it with the state as a "business" to protect it from ever being disturbed. While Falwell went off to Bible school and returned to become famous, Gene stuck to his country roots, working as a mechanic, a farmer, and a handyman.

Gene's life is instructive of what an anomaly Jerry Falwell was in a town like Lynchburg. Carey's gas station, boarded up and frozen in time, still sits in front of Gene's house. The neighborhood is dotted with ramshackle brick cottages and 1950s-era wooden shacks, much as it was when Jerry Falwell grew up there. Gene lives with his wife Joanne, a cat named Lucy, and a hound dog named Blackie. He owns a sixty-three-family mobile home park, collecting rent from his tenants, and serving as the community's maintenance man. It's a good living—he takes home about $100,000 a year, Gene says. He lays gravel driveways and performs plumbing and electrical work for his tenants. Gene also keeps two backhoes on his property, which he occasionally uses to dig graves for neighbors who have suffered a death in the family.

He charges nine hundred dollars a plot, but sometimes performs the service pro bono.

Carey Falwell never talked much about his shooting of Garland to Gene or Jerry. Just thinking about it makes Gene wince. "Please don't dredge all that up," he says. "It oughta just stay buried."

LYNCHBURG is a town where, historically, business moguls haven't been afraid to throw their weight around, especially when it came to fellow businesses. A stunning example came in the mid-1960s, when the editorial policies of Lynchburg's two newspapers, *The News* and *Daily Advance*, came under scrutiny from the national news media. What caused the attention was a refusal by the papers' general manager, Carter Glass III, to run black death notices. The papers often mocked public figures like preacher Rev. Virgil Wood, calling him a "local Negro agitator."[1] Harold Leggett, secretary-treasurer of the Leggett department-store chain, had a letter co-signed by seventy-one (mostly white) business leaders, demanding the antiblack policies stop. Leggett was one of the papers' biggest advertisers. The letter went out to nearly every household in Lynchburg, thanks to a Sears customer mailing list contributed by a manager at Sears' downtown store. Glass capitulated. *Life* magazine covered the story with the headline, "When City Bites Newspaper, That's News."[2]

In Lynchburg, Jerry Falwell had more wins under his belt in business than in politics. When Falwell tried to get annual tax breaks of $250,000 for Liberty in 1986, the city council balked. He threatened to leave Lynchburg and to move some of his ministries to Atlanta. "We must be the only university in America that pays real-estate taxes," grumbled Mark DeMoss at the time. The city eventually complied, asking the Virginia State Assembly to authorize the tax breaks, which it did.

Most of Falwell's battles with the city involved rezoning. When Ericsson announced that its giant cell phone plant might be sold to Jerry Falwell Ministries, some members of the planning commission panicked. The Ericsson plant was one of the biggest parcels of land in the city zoned for manufacturing. Its sale to a nonprofit would mean a permanent loss of tax revenue. The trouble was, Ericsson had tried to sell the land for over a year, with no takers. When the *News & Advance* opposed the sale to Falwell's ministry, Falwell again used his pulpit to strike back. During a Sunday morning service, Falwell denounced the paper's position, calling for editor Joe Stinett to be sacked. "You can't box with God," warned Falwell. "Jerry was so angry he banned the sale of our paper on his campus for two years," says Stinett. After Hobby Lobby gifted the Ericsson building to Thomas Road, Jerry Jr. sought the widest possible zoning—B5—for the building, which would allow an ice skating rink and restaurants. The planning commission recommended a far more restrictive B1 designation. Jerry Jr. prepared a list of "proffers," a list of promises made in return for a more permissive use. But he bypassed planners and sneaked them directly to members of the city council, who have final say. Jerry Jr. got the B5 zoning he wanted.

Almost singlehandedly, Jerry Jr. is also the man who paved the way for big-box discounters like Wal-Mart and Sam's Club to move into town, most of whom have dropped anchor along Wards Road next to the Liberty campus. It was not the city, but Jerry Jr.

who lured them with Liberty's growing student and faculty population and with good deals on land alongside roads bordering Liberty. That was irksome to then city planning director Rachel Flynn, Harvard grad and a foe of big-box outlets. Flynn complained that a much smaller percentage of money made by superstores, as opposed to local mom-and-pops, gets recycled to the local economy. Small businesses tend to hire local accountants, lawyers, and suppliers; big-box retailers let their corporate heirarchy handle such needs. Another criticism is esthetic: big-box architecture is just plain cookie-cutter ugly. During her eight years as a planner in Lynchburg, Flynn fought with Falwell over the placement of exit ramps near Liberty and the protection of a stream near a new Cracker Barrel. Falwell denounced Flynn too, from his pulpit, likening her policies to Communist central planning.

For years, Flynn and other Lynchburg planners have tried to sell developers in town on "new urbanism," a planning philosophy popular in the 1980s, which promoted mixed-use buildings in varying sizes and a diversity of smaller, locally owned businesses. The city's Wyndhurst development, in southeast Lynchburg, is its best example. Wyndhurst started as four hundred acres of open fields; city planners used a unique zoning grid to lure forty small businesses and franchises to the area, where they opened up shop in low-rise buildings. The development harkens back to the Charlie Falwell era, when city dwellers walked to the corner restaurant, bank, or haberdasher. Businesses operated on the ground floor and owners lived in apartments on the second floor. Wyndhurst revived that vision, luring local banks, real-estate and life-insurance companies alongside jewelers, beauty salons, a dry cleaners, cigar sellers, and purveyors of golf equipment. Wyndhurst also has a dozen restaurants and a retirement home.

Contrast this with the retail boom around Liberty, populated by the likes of Wal-Mart, Target, Kohl's, and Sam's Club, who chose sites based on highway access. The only way to meet the kind of volume Wal-Mart needs to be viable in a community like Lynchburg is to have people-moving mechanisms (highways) which can propel vast numbers of consumers to parking lots big enough to accommodate them. Such a model collides with the logic of a university, which is planned centrally and whose focus isn't moving them around, but keeping them in one place. Big-box developments don't preclude diversity, of course—Wards Road has dozens of chain restaurants, from Cracker Barrel to Bob Evans. But few are locally owned.

Chris Doyle, a broker for CB Richard Ellis in Richmond and Jerry Jr.'s real-estate point man, is no fan of new urbanism. "Retailing thrives on a herd mentality," says Doyle. "Anchor stores drive people in and selection keeps them there. That's why new urbanism doesn't work in Lynchburg. We don't have the density of a New York City or a Washington, D.C., to support lots of little shops."

Doyle is a stocky Irish Catholic who has worked closely over the last decade on development deals with the Falwells, especially Jerry Jr. They rarely discuss religion, but Doyle once shocked Jerry Jr. by arriving at his home on Ash Wednesday with a gray smudge on his forehead. "He looked at me like I was a nut," said Doyle, until Doyle explained the origins of Palm Sunday, the creation of ashes, and how they signal the start of the Lenten season. Jerry Jr. learned much more from Doyle. It was Doyle who walked Jerry Jr. through the labyrinthine world of local zoning procedures, learning about traffic flows and signalization, how sewage and power grids flow, when to issue proffers, and why it's important to know the difference between intermittent versus ephemeral streams. He would learn from Doyle how to lay the groundwork and do the grunt work necessary to re-zone property to commercial uses favored by developers.

In leading this big-box stampede, Doyle and Jerry Jr. have produced a curious hometown rivalry. As the city places its bets on the old, northern part of the city, the center of economic gravity keeps tilting south. That giant sucking sound is coming from the vast stretches of land being developed at breakneck speed around Liberty University.

Since the mid-1990s the city has spent millions trying to revive Lynchburg's historic downtown. Joan Foster, who succeeded Carl Hutcherson as Lynchburg mayor, campaigned on a downtown re-development platform. The city is spending millions to upgrade roads and to build pedestrian arcades at major tourist areas like Monument Terrace, Ninth Street, and Riverfront Park. There's the $23 million Bluffwalk Center, comprising a boutique-style 44-room hotel in the old Craddock-Terry Shoe factory and a new restaurant and brewery; a $30-million restoration of the historic Academy of Music Theatre; $17 million for a new courthouse and post office; a $12-million renovation of three buildings on Main Street to construct sixty-seven loft apartments, and a $3-million improvement to sidewalks, lamps, benches, and trees at the base of Ninth Street, where John Lynch once ran his ferry. "For every dollar we invest we'll get three to four dollars back," says Foster.

Lynchburg's bid to revitalize its downtown is what convinced Jenny West, a sixty-ish blonde antiques dealer to buy the Norvell-Otey mansion on Federal Hill near downtown in 1995. She was fascinated with its history and thought she could transform the elegant mansion into a small hotel to tap the coming economic boom. The home had been built by Capt. William Norvell in 1815 on land he acquired from John Lynch. Norvell was a friend of Jefferson's who dined with the former president when he rode into Lynchburg.

When West bought the house it was being run as a beauty salon by two young men who had decorated the ground floor with lawn furniture. West turned it into a high-end bed-and-breakfast, cramming every floor with antiques and silver. She keeps her mammoth silver collection a secret, revealing only that she has enough to have recently catered a wedding for 125 people with full service. She's fortunate to have a side business: it's been twelve years since she purchased the Norvell-Otey house and West is still waiting for the economic revitalization to arrive. At times, downtown Lynchburg seems as dead as Liberty Village. In the middle of the workweek its streets are almost deserted. Workers commute to offices downtown and leave at the end of the day; they do not linger at bars, restaurants, or nightclubs. Very few such establishments exist. There are boarded-up storefronts along the very heart of Main Street. Not a single major public parking garage exists downtown—there is no need for one.

In 2007, Lynchburg collected $70 million in tax receipts. Nearly half of that comes from businesses near a single, two-mile stretch of road running along Liberty's western border. Yet, most of the city's economic development dollars are going to revitalize downtown, which produces just a fraction of tax receipts. The disparity causes Doyle to ask, "Why does ninety-eight cents on the dollar go to something that's not throwing off nearly the same return as what you have around the Liberty campus?"

Liberty's land is in the middle of what Doyle calls a "trade triangle." Lynchburg is the biggest city in the United States without access to an interstate. But the ring of roads around Liberty's campus—highways 29, 460, and 501—make it fertile ground for developers eager to lure not just Lynchburg's 64,000 residents, but the area's larger metropolitan population of 240,000.

Even Doyle concedes there isn't much retail room left. He thinks the city can accommodate one more giant shopping center, perhaps another 900,000 square feet of retail space. His theory will soon be tested. Two new malls are under construction near Liberty, each nearing one million square feet apiece. The biggest, Lakeside Center, is referred to by the local press as a "mercantile juggernaut," and is expected to bring in $10 million in annual tax revenue and to add 1200 jobs. The other, Crossroads Colonnade, is a 760,000-square-foot mall, hotel, and water park on land belonging to Liberty.

Jerry Jr. can see the day when Liberty hits a total enrollment of 50,000. There may be no room left for shopping centers, but Liberty's expansion will head north along the 460 corridor, a stretch of road renamed "Jerry Falwell Parkway" by the Virginia Legislature in 2008. Jerry Jr. expects to encounter the same kind of flak he dealt with in the fall of 2007 to rezone a mere three acres of land within the Lynchburg city limits, a spillover of a 138-acre parcel in neighboring Campbell County. The county had no problem giving Jerry Jr. the zoning change he wanted, but the city balked. Lynchburg's planners were trying to exact traffic and environmental concessions over the entire development by using their tiny foothold in the project as leverage, he says.

The move so angered Jerry Jr. that he is moving ahead with a plan started by his father to register Liberty students to vote in

Ward 3, the section of town in which Liberty resides. His idea is to turn the incoming Liberty student body into a local voting bloc, which could target hostile members of the city council and reshape Lynchburg's city government with Liberty-friendly officials who will send more economic development dollars south. What makes Jerry Jr. think Liberty students would take such political action? Their pocketbooks. The next time a major proposal for, say, a pedestrian bridge from campus over Wards Road is shot down by the city council, Jerry Jr. could legitimately argue to students that its defeat means that the university will have to shoulder the cost of building it, sparking higher tuition fees. It's an idea harkening to the leverage Jerry Jr.'s grandfather Carey had in the late 1920s, with his fuel oil and bootlegging businesses. The mere threat of such a large voting bloc is enough to give Jerry Jr. more local political power than his father ever had. Mayor Foster appears to be concerned. "I would hope Jerry Jr. comes to us first before moving ahead with something like this," she says delicately.

9. FALWELL 2.0

I N the shifting sands of the Religious Right, Jerry Falwell's footprints are still visible. One might thank Falwell for the fact that virtually every 2008 presidential candidate has a religious outreach director, or that conservative Christians now openly apply their values as a litmus test for those seeking public office. Or even that Hillary Rodham Clinton now wears a crucifix.

One might also thank Falwell and the Religious Right for the fact that every U.S. President since Jimmy Carter has professed to have had a born-again experience. There are now more evangelical Christians in the three branches of U.S. government than at any time in history.[1] In 1963 only about 100 churches in the U.S. had more than 1,000 members. Today there are 750 churches with over 2,000 members.[2]

Management guru Peter Drucker believed that while the

corporation was the most significant institution to arise in the early twentieth century, megachurches like Falwell's were the most significant sociological phenomenon in the second half of the century. Half of all charitable donations in the U.S. each year go to churches; one-third of all the time volunteered by Americans go to churches.

Men of God inspire trust. Former Arkansas Governor and Baptist minister Mike Huckabee's win in the 2008 Iowa caucuses "is a good example of the legacy of Jerry Falwell," says John Green, senior fellow at the Pew Center on Religion and Public Life. "Falwell made it appropriate to bring religious values into the political realm. That's a radical idea that has endured."

Will Falwell's legacy be enough of a difference in the 2008 election? "What we're going to have to say is, 'Folks, this is the fish. We just have to eat it and spit out the bones,'" says Godwin. That kind of compromising drives rock-ribbed Christians crazy, but they're the ones who count. "The juice that motivates the conservative movement comes from its religious branch," says Godwin. "If we're not motivated, you can kiss the victory away."

To some of the conservative old guard, that wouldn't be such a bad idea. At the Values Voters Summit in Salt Lake City in September 2007, Godwin found himself cornered by his old Moral Majority colleague, Richard Viguerie. Viguerie sits, politically speaking, just to the right of Attila the Hun. Viguerie had heard that Godwin was chaperoning Jonathan and Jerry Jr. to meet with the Republican candidates, including a private audience with Mitt Romney at his home during the summit. Viguerie had some advice for Godwin.

"Ron, you gotta train those boys," said Viguerie. "They're green and they're naive."

Godwin shot Viguerie a bemused look. "Okay, what am I supposed to tell 'em?"

"Tell them it would be best for Republicans to lose the presidential election crushingly and horribly. Tell them that the party needs to be burned to the ground because this last administration is so corrupt and god-awful that it has got to be taught a lesson."

Godwin gave Viguerie a look of disbelief. "Richard, gimme a break. You want eight more years before we can bring justice and light back to the country? I don't think so." Godwin later put the conversation in context. "My conservative friends make fantastic guerillas. They know how to raise hell. But to actually make measured judgments essential to governance, well, we're a bit short."

In the summer of 2007, Jonathan, Jerry Jr., and Godwin met with nearly every Republican presidential hopeful. The trio was not an easy audience. "Most of the candidates can't talk our talk. They don't belong to our subculture," says Godwin. "People who do that superficially, like John McCain, fail miserably."

Godwin and Jerry Jr. met then-candidate Fred Thompson and his buxom, blonde wife Jeri for two hours. Thompson leaned back in his chair and looked squarely at Jerry Jr., serenely reeling off a list of titles he's held in the Senate. His baritone twang had the reassuringly quality of someone who had been there, done that. He had served two terms in the U.S. Senate and was junior counsel to the Senate Watergate Committee. It was Thompson who had suggested to then-Nixon aide Howard Baker the bombshell questions that brought Nixon down. Thompson was a part of living history. "It was as if he was suggesting he deserved the presidency based solely on his résumé," said Godwin.

Jeri Thompson interrupted her husband, saying that she rarely offered her two cents on religious matters but wanted to get something off her chest. Just a few months earlier Focus on the Family chief James Dobson had questioned Thompson's Christian credentials. Dobson professed he was misquoted and misinterpreted. But the damage had been done, said Jeri. The criticism hurt. "How can a man who doesn't even know Fred pass judgment on him like that?" she asked, her eyes misting up. Jerry Jr. liked Thompson— "He reminds me of Ronald Reagan." Jerry Jr. empathized with Thompson's wife, asking, "How can we help get the word out to set the record straight?"

The meeting put Godwin in a sour mood. "Sometimes Jerry Jr. will pull the trigger and jump before he consults with anyone. He makes up his mind fast. It keeps me up at nights sometimes. Jerry is taken by Thompson. Jonathan and I are not."

In early May of 2007, Jonathan and Godwin caught a plane to Manhattan for lunch with Rudolph Giuliani at his campaign office just a few blocks from the World Trade Center site. Giuliani was in a buoyant mood, heaping praise on Thomas Road and Liberty University. "I respect you. I respect your values and your point of view. If I were president, you'd have an open door," he said, spearing a forkful of salad. They managed to discuss the most prickly issue of all without using the word itself: abortion. "Let's be honest," said Giuliani. "I can't pull a Romney and flip-flop. That would kill me."

After lunch, Jonathan and Giuliani spent a few minutes alone while Godwin chatted with his aides. Jonathan never expected Giuliani to promise to fight against abortion, but maybe he could help someone who would. Jonathan knew that the power of vice presidents has been gaining in the last few administrations. Al Gore's mini-fiefdom during the Clinton years has been likened to that of a prime minister. Dick Cheney has a national security staff almost parallel in structure to George Bush's. Jonathan thought about whether a similar power base might be forged for his own candidate, Mike Huckabee.

Jonathan said to Giuliani: "You know you've got issues with evangelicals. We've got issues with you. But you've got to figure out how to get us on board. One thing that could go a long way is to put someone like Mike Huckabee in place. If you can bring someone like Huckabee on board it'll signal you're going to move a little to the right. It will also set Mike Huckabee up eight years from now." Giuliani told Jonathan he would do it, says Godwin. It's just the kind of compromise Jonathan's father might have brokered. A few months later Huckabee came to speak to students at Liberty. After the talk Jerry Jr. unexpectedly endorsed Huckabee's candidacy. "I believe with all my heart that if my father had witnessed Governor Huckabee's surge in the polls and his ascension to first place in Iowa, he would have endorsed Governor Huckabee without hesitation." In fact, Falwell had already made his selection. Shortly before his death he secretly told Newt Gingrich he would back him if he ran.

Today, the Religious Right has reverted to its pre-Falwell fractured state of every-man-for-himself endorsements. In 2007, Pat Robertson threw his support behind Giuliani; Paul Weyrich endorsed Mitt Romney. Jonathan says he isn't concerned about such splintering. "Dad started the Religious Right. But I don't think that in today's world there's a place for a single person to lead this movement. You have a lot of other people out there now—Tony Perkins, James

Dobson. There's not a need for dad today like there was thirty years ago."

That's not a winning argument with Art Williams, Liberty's billionaire backer. "I think that's a bunch of crap," he says. "We need a Jerry Falwell now more than ever. All the spokesmen we have today are just too nice. They're a bunch of dad gum mealymouths," says Williams. The campaign of 2008 is the first election he can remember that he's not excited about. "I don't like any of the candidates. The Democrats are going to win. They're just gonna clean house."

What Jerry Jr. and Jonathan face today is not so much a world divided by a Religious Right and secular left, but the rise of the religious left and the secular right. Barack Obama and Hillary Rodham Clinton are not writing off values voters, they are embracing them. Younger evangelicals are less concerned about social conservatism than in past generations. John Green describes a new generation of evangelical Christians who want to tackle a broader agenda. But he also points out that diversity among evangelicals was always there, it is only now becoming more visible. "One pastor told me that if the Bible applies to sex, why doesn't it then apply to war and peace, and the environment?" Some mainline Christian conservatives are actually voicing confidence in science, particularly when it comes to global warming. That infuriated Falwell. In a February 2007 sermon, he said that evangelicals who take up the fight against global warming represent "Satan's attempt to redirect the church's primary focus," which is spreading the Gospel.

Had Falwell lived much beyond his seventy-three years, he would likely be battling conservatives themselves. He was a die-hard

George Bush supporter, even though polls taken by the Pew Research Center showed that evangelicals long ago lost faith in the president. What was once a 90 percent approval rating for Bush by white evangelicals had dropped to just under 45 percent in early 2007.[3] The conservative movement today is constituted by perhaps two-thirds economic hawks and one-third social hawks. Economic conservatives can't stand Huckabee. Social conservatives can't stand McCain. But someone will have to eat the fish.

Falwell knew how to do this yet still seem uncompromising. In the 2006 U.S. Senate race in Virginia, where Falwell's longtime ally, George Allen, watched his campaign implode over his clumsy use of the term "macaca" to describe a young man working for his opponent, Falwell may have played a role in pulling the rug out from Allen as he watched Allen's poll ratings melt. In an interview with this writer on Forbes.com, Falwell awarded Democrat James Webb, then running against Allen, an "A-" as a candidate, practically endorsing him, yet keeping his praise measured by explaining that Webb gets such a grade simply for having held the position of secretary of the navy under Reagan. The comment was picked up by political reporters and dozens of Beltway political blogs. Webb won the race.

In his first sermon just five days after his father's death, Jonathan likened his father's passing to what happened when God responded to the death of Moses. God dispatched Joshua to carry on the Gospel. "Casual Christianity has never changed the world. Convenient Christianity has never changed the world. Comfortable Christianity has never changed the world. Only Committed Christians do."

Jonathan is embarking on a growth strategy called, "Joshua 2."

It is a remake of his father's saturation canvassing back in the late 1950s. He wants to add 5,000 people to his Sunday school; double the attendance of his 24,000-member congregation; plant 500 churches around the country and send out 500 more missionaries around the world. "There are 240,000 people who live within thirty minutes of where I sit," says Jonathan. "Only 18 percent of them are in church on any given Sunday. Some of them are unsaved, but many of them *are* saved—they just don't think the church is important or relevant. We've broken down every neighborhood, every street, within thirty miles of here. We can look at a four-block, micro-neighborhood, identify a member of Thomas Road who lives there, and print out a map. We'll tell them we want them to be responsible for reaching out to their own little neighborhoods."

Jonathan has fewer tools to grow his church, a local entity, than Jerry Jr. has to grow his school, which casts a national footprint. Falwell Inc. is now driven by a school, not a church. In 2008, Liberty will report revenues of $128 million. It is now debt free, thanks to the $29 million in life insurance Falwell designated to pay off Liberty's remaining IOUs (he also directed $6 million toward the church's debt, which still has $14 million to pay off in construction costs for its new sanctuary). Liberty now has 10,700 residential students, up from 4,500 in 2001.

"It's true that Liberty is debt free," says Godwin. "But it's also endowment poor." That latter point has preoccupied the Falwells ever since Liberty's debt crisis eased in the late 1990s. For a time Falwell and Jerry Jr. saw their 5,000 acres on the mountain as the solution. They considered restaurants, condominiums, and hotels. They talked about building $20 million in amenities, from a golf course and ski resort, to an equestrian center and a 60-foot dam (to create a 100-acre lake), which would enhance the value of the acreage adjoining these developments. Golf-course architect Robert Trent Jones Jr. trooped in one day to survey the mountain's potential, as have dozens of other developers.

Now Jerry Jr. sees the mountain less as a vehicle for monetizing and more as a campus amenity for Liberty students. The thirty miles of biking trails Jerry Jr. bulldozed on the mountain have lured scores of bikers and brought glowing write-ups in national press like *Outside* magazine and *The New York Times*. When Jerry Jr. and Jonathan visited President Bush with their families in the Oval Office in the summer of 2007, Bush had one thing on his mind. "All he wanted to do is talk about mountain biking and the trails we opened up," says Jerry Jr. Presidential aides have since asked for maps and directions to the trails.

Liberty has $163 million pledged to its endowment in the form of wills, bequests, trusts, and gift annuities, most from members of the church. About $90 million of that is in cash. Jerry Jr. is at work on scads of other ideas. A former Detroit auto engineer donated a design to Liberty, which would decrease the cost of making printed circuit boards. Jerry Jr. filed a patent for the process and plans to market the idea, estimating it could be worth north of $250 million. He admits the figure is "speculative."

At the Planned Giving office of Jerry Falwell Ministries is a U.S. map on the wall with pushpins in every state, denoting the origins of gifts. The name of the office is a misnomer. Most gifts are not planned; only about 20 percent of contributions that arrive are expected. They are not bombshell contributions like Art Williams's $70 million or David Green's donation of a $26 million cell-phone building. They are largely noncash contributions, which have included a big-game trophy collection donated by a retired dentist (the thirty-two species included a large black bear, goats, and caribou); a California avocado farm; a field of natural gas wells; a $1.2 million Piper Meridian airplane and $300,000 in gold ingots.[4]

One cash gift in 2004 required some artful tactics to accept it. A woman in Arizona wanted to give Falwell's ministry $50,000 in cash—money she had been squirreling away in her home for over a decade. As a condition of her donation, she insisted the money be hand-delivered to the ministry—not wired or deposited at a local bank branch. Falwell dispatched his planned giving officer, Everett Foutz, to make the pickup, telling him to put the money in a briefcase. When Foutz arrived at the donor's home, he was given a white cardbox box filled with $50,000 in $100 bills. Foutz didn't like thinking about trying to bring $50,000 cash in his carry-on luggage. So Jerry Jr. suggested Foutz divide the money five ways, putting $10,000 apiece in five garbage bags, and shipping each one separately via Federal Express. All five arrived.[5]

Over the years, other unplanned gifts came when Falwell managed to dupe his enemies into helping him fund-raise millions without them ever knowing it. One of the best examples is the dividends Falwell collected from a *Hustler* magazine parody of a Campari ad depicting Falwell's "first time" as having been an incestuous relationship in an outhouse with his mother. Falwell filed a defamation suit against its publisher, Larry Flynt, for $50 million. Over the next five years Flynt lost the case, appealed, then lost again (the case later figured prominently in the 1996 movie, *The People vs. Larry Flynt*). Conservative Christians considered it their own cause celebre and urged Falwell, in letters and contributions, to continue his fight against one of the nation's most prominent pornographers.

When the case finally reached the U.S. Supreme Court, the jury verdict favoring Falwell was overturned by a unanimous, 8-0 vote. The court found that public figures like Falwell are not entitled to be compensated for emotional distress intentionally inflicted on them if not done with a reckless disregard for the truth. Falwell could not meet that standard. A few weeks after the decision Falwell flew out to California to pay a visit to Flynt with an idea: although the case had been decided, why not continue the debate on a national tour, he suggested. Flynt agreed; the pair would debate the merits of the case on college campuses, and in television and radio studios. One such appearance came in 1988 on *Larry King Live*. After the pair debated the morality of the court's decision, Falwell got a call from one of his staff back in Lynchburg. A Florida real-estate developer had been watching the show and called to request information on how to wire a one-million-dollar cash contribution to Falwell's church.

Like other megachurch pastors, Falwell's religious ventures grew more or less in line with the media exposure he received. "Do you realize that every Sunday it is possible for any preacher in America, through the miracle of the media, to preach in one sermon to more people than heard Paul preach in all of his life?" Falwell once said. "The media has done more to turn this country toward God than any one aspect of the propagation of the gospel in this century." In the 1980s and 1990s Falwell appeared on *Larry King Live* as often as once a month, and in one year clocked eleven appearances on ABC's *Nightline*. It may seem ridiculous to accuse a children's television character, Tinky Winky, of promoting homosexuality, as a

Falwell publication did in 1999. But that single accusation caused a mountain of publicity—1,600 stories in newspapers, magazines, and the airwaves noted the controversy.

Liberty's growth sport has prompted Jerry Jr. to begin lobbying the city to build a civic center, promising that Liberty would be a prime tenant (the city is reluctant to take on the huge debt that would be required to do it). One site under consideration is the land where Chase McCool's dormitory now sits, overlooking the southern end of Candler's Mountain. A sticking point is whether alcohol would be served at the venue. Another project that's a surer bet: Doc's Diner, a restaurant named for Falwell scheduled to open in 2008. It will be stocked with personal belongings and memorabilia, and most certainly will be alcohol-free.

Jerry Falwell's death has brought good tithings for his business ventures. Besides the giant life-insurance payouts and a stampede of new members to Thomas Road, Liberty received a donation of local real estate worth $2.5 million from entrepreneur Sherwin Cook and a shopping center worth $15 million.

Perhaps the toughest spot for Jerry Jr. and Jonathan to fill is the football coach-style pep talk Falwell gave to those attending "College for a Weekend," an event that drew 1,828 high-school seniors the last time Falwell hosted it in the spring of 2007. At these gatherings Falwell explained the rationale for attending a school like Liberty. You could see expressions of wonderment, admiration, sometimes disbelief. But he never bored them. "My father was the biggest distributor of illegal whiskey in this part of the country," boomed Falwell, describing his own family history in mesmerizing detail. He described the Liberty campus as a citadel for God. "Jesus Christ is the central personality at this university. You're on a radical piece of property," he intoned. "You can't become a nuclear scientist or an architect here. But spend four years at Liberty and you will have a vision you can take to get those degrees. To get a vision you have to have access to your heart. You'll get that here. You'll get your anchor. Then go on and become whatever you want."

Falwell inspired them to think cosmically; to get beyond their concerns about degree programs and double majors. If you took away Falwell's references to an inerrant Bible and broadsides against gays and abortion, his rallies would resemble human potential seminars. Falwell built Christian organizations not just to enshrine values he believed in, raise money, or reap political change. His entrepreneurial zeal was rooted in a personal catharsis over the agonies of his childhood. The life and death struggles of his university and church were battles for his own identity. Would he emulate the entrepreneurial Carey Falwell of the 1920s, a self-made mogul whose businesses controlled much of Lynchburg, or Carey of the late 1930s, a broken man destroyed by alcoholism and financial ruin?

IT'S a good time to be in education. The "echo boom" delivered a record 14 percent rise in college enrollments in 2007. Admissions at Christian schools jumped 64 percent between 1990 and 2003 (double the growth rate at public schools). Students at these schools are not interested in simply becoming pastors or church builders: Among the top majors at conservative Christian schools is business. Distance education degrees at Christian schools are far cheaper than their secular counterparts. An online MBA at Duke University costs $107,000; at Liberty it costs $10,260.

Liberty's competition is the five hundred Christian colleges, schools, and distance learning degrees now jostling for echo-boom students. Many are fledging enterprises; a few are behemoths with deep-pocketed angels. Domino's Pizza founder Thomas Monaghan has donated or pledged $285 million to build Ave Maria, a four-year Catholic school just outside tony Naples, Florida—and construct an entire town around it.

One of Ave Maria's centerpiece institutions will be its law school; its founders have been studying the Liberty model. Liberty's inaugural law school class of 2007 scored an 89-percent national pass rate, vaulting it to the top 20 percent of all ABA-approved law schools. Law schools in Virginia average a rate of 70 percent.

Liberty's biggest success, of course, is its distance learning program. In 2007, Liberty's online enrollment hit a record 27,000 students. It is now among the top ten online schools in America. Its courses net $30 million on $72 million in revenue in 2007. How does it generate so much cash? An instructor for an eight-week online course at Liberty costs Godwin $2,800. If that course is sold to forty students, the return for Liberty is $20,000. Apply that math to an entire degree program—Liberty offers thirty-four. All this makes the value of Liberty's online curricula at least $400 million. It explains some of the unusual visitors to Ron Godwin's office in the summer of 2007. They arrived in Learjets and Gulfstream IIIs, carrying executives of competing online education ventures shopping for an equity stake, or maybe an outright purchase.

It took Jerry Falwell thirty-five years to grow his residential campus to 10,000 students. It took Ron Godwin two years to grow Liberty's online program from 9,000 to 27,000 students. Godwin's goal is to boost online enrollment, regardless of outside investments, to 70,000, which would make it worth one billion dollars. To do it, Liberty will go south. Some 100 million people identify themselves as evangelicals in Latin and South America (60 million in Brazil, 40 million more across 19 other countries). A majority have dropped out of school before reaching the ninth grade. The result is a giant pool of uneducated blue collar workers. The market is there; what's missing is broad access to computers and mechanisms to pay for such courses, says Godwin.

A faith-based campus is one thing, but how is Christian faith conveyed in an online course? Unlike the residential campus, there is no required chapel attendance. The 250 adjunct faculty who teach Liberty's online courses are required to accept a "statement of faith." There is an online spiritual service, where Liberty faith advisers answer questions about faith and doctrine. But some of those adjuncts are in California and Texas. Residential students attend Christian convocation three times a week. That would be hard to duplicate for a student in New York taking online classes from a school in Central Virginia whose instructors are on the West Coast.

Liberty's financial future looks safe, for now. But will the conservative nature of its residential campus survive the absence of its founder? Falwell was obsessed by the question. The possibility that Liberty's mission would someday be watered down, its curriculum softened of its fundamentalist fiber, kept Falwell up at night. "The history of American education is filled with universities begun as Christian schools that turn into mainstream liberal colleges," he once warned Jonathan.

Liberty may be a bastion of fundamentalism, but it is surrounded by liberal forces. One of the most popular Liberty student hangouts is Macado's, a smoke-filled Hard Rock Café–style diner on the very border of campus. It breaks every Baptist rule in the book. Customers smoke and drink beneath photos of Elton John and the female rock band Vixen. Rock music churns and *Rolling Stone* magazine covers featuring Bill Clinton and Al Gore adorn the walls. Alcohol is served by Liberty students—they're not allowed to drink but can make $500 a week helping others tie one on.

A few doors down from Macado's is a hotel frequented by Liberty student parents, which employs transgender staff at the front desk. And although it may come as a shock to Mat Staver, the editor of the university newspaper, Jenni Thurman, keeps a purple Harry Potter banner affixed to her office wall. "It's not witchcraft," she says, rolling her eyes. "It's just a story."

What will ultimately protect the orthodoxy of Jerry Falwell's university is a business relationship. When the church took over the Ericsson building Falwell had a unique contract drawn up. It allows the church to lease most of its Ericsson building space to Liberty for one dollar a year for ninety-nine years (with an option to renew). By making the school a tenant of the church, Falwell codified a relationship that will, in theory, keep the school true to its fundamentalist values. Liberty's thirty-five-member board has no deans or faculty members. It is packed with pastors and local Christian businessfolks.

"Dad set it up so that the church will forever be the rudder that guides the university," says Jonathan. "He said that if Liberty ever turns to the left, members of the board should fire everyone and shut the place down. The nuclear option exists. They will use it if they have to." Spoken like a true fundamentalist.

ACKNOWLEDGMENTS

The person to whom I owe the biggest debt of gratitude for making this book a reality is Jerry Falwell Jr. In what was the most difficult time of his life, he took many hours away from the escalating demands on his time to explain the financial roller-coaster ride he, his father, and brother, Jonathan, were on for a decade.

I owe a special debt to Ron Godwin, Falwell's closest aide, whose institutional history of the Falwell family businesses was invaluable. I appreciate the many hours of time he gave to answer my questions about events that occurred over a span of thirty years. Jonathan Falwell also deserves thanks for generously offering his time and reflections during what was an equally difficult hour for him and his family. I could not have been luckier than to have Tom Post guide the original story on Jerry Falwell and Liberty University in *Forbes,* which served as the basis of this book. He is a brilliant, demanding editor and a compassionate mentor. I would probably not have done this book without the encouragement of Stewart Pinkerton, *Forbes*'s deputy managing editor and one of the lions of business journalism. I am hugely grateful to *Forbes* editor William Baldwin, who granted my leave of absence to do this project.

The Jones Memorial Library in Lynchburg, Virginia, is one of the best research libraries I have ever visited. The assistance from its staff was so stellar, I always hated to leave. I am also indebted to the smarts and savvy of the *Forbes* library staff, especially Anne Mintz and Sue Radlauer, who didn't seem to mind the temporary satellite office I created in their midst. Among those who gave me editorial advice for this book was Mary Ellen Egan, *Forbes*'s chief of reporters, whose instincts for journalistic storytelling shined in her valuable feedback.

I owe a huge slice of gratitude to Phil Revzin, St. Martin's Press senior editor, whose supremely smart suggestions gave this project its bearings, and to assistant editor Jenness Crawford. My agent at William Morris, Mel Berger, shaped the original proposal with a flurry of brutal but brilliant sagelike comments.

A very special thanks to Aura Levitas, my daughter's godmother, for making her beautiful home in Southampton, Long Island, available to me—it's a place where writing about anything is a pleasure. I thank my friends on both coasts for allowing me to abandon all contact with them for nearly a year. My mom, Gwen, and sister, Claudia, were more patient with my long periods of monklike solitude than I could have asked for.

To all the faculty and students who let me become part of their work during my trips to Lynchburg in the summer and fall of 2007, I am deeply indebted to you. They are not used to having journalists rummage through their offices, eat at their dining halls, and monitor their classes. But they put up with me. I am indebted to Debate Coach Michael Hall for letting me spend time at his debate camp, and Liberty Law School Dean Mat Staver for allowing me to sit in on his incoming class's first week as student barristers.

Other key people at Liberty who shared time with me include Elmer Towns, Lee Beaumont, and Jim Moon. Lynchburg Police Chief Charles Bennett gets a special nod for finding time to discuss the town's fascinating history. I wish him well in his forthcoming assignment in Iraq, where he will serve as a senior adviser to U.S. forces attempting to build a national police force.

My biggest thanks goes to my family, who put up with my annoying habit of seeking out the nearest Starbucks everywhere we went in 2007, from Hamden, Connecticut, to Carmel, California, so that I could plug in and bang out my chapters.

I owe the most to my wife, Martha, who in the midst of her own year of profound challenges found creative ways to give me the time I needed to do this book. For months, my six-year-old daughter, Lorelei, put up with a sleep-deprived father, whose mountains of books and research posed a constant threat of burying her. Thank you, Lorelei.

NOTES

INTRODUCTION

1. Peter Carlson, "Witness to the Gospel According to Falwell," *Washington Post,* May 16, 2007: C1.

I. A SMALL-TOWN KILLING

1. Jean M. West, "Tobacco and Slavery: The Vile Weed," *Slavery in America,* 3, http://www.slaveryinamerica.org/history/hs_es _tobacco_slavery.htm.

2. Ibid., 7.

3. James M. Elson, *Lynchburg, Virginia: The First 200 Years, 1786 to 1986* (Warwick House Publishers, 2004), 20.

4. Darrell Laurent, *A City Unto Itself* (Lynchburg, VA: News & Advance, 1997), 7.

5. Elson, *Lynchburg, Virginia,* 52.

6. Laurent, *A City Unto Itself,* 66.

7. West, "Tobacco and Slavery," 4.

8. Elson, *Lynchburg, Virginia,* 64.

9. W. Asbury Christian, *Lynchburg and Its People* (J. P. Bell Co., 1900), 83.

10. Elson, *Lynchburg, Virginia,* 34.

11. Ibid., 28.

12. Ibid., 139.

13. Laurent, *A City Unto Itself,* 18.

2. VERBAL VIGILANTES

1. Jerry Falwell, *Falwell: An Autobiography* (Lynchburg, VA: Liberty House Publishers, 1997), 62.

2. Ibid., 64.

3. Ibid., 63.

4. Ibid., 64.

5. No byline, "Table Phones Paris Novelty," *The News,* July 24, 1929: 24.

6. Falwell, *Falwell: An Autobiography,* 58.

7. Ibid., 84.

8. Ibid., 82.

9. Ibid., 89.

10. Ibid., 113.

11. Ibid., 107.

12. Ibid., 120.

13. Ibid., 139.

14. Jerry Falwell and Elmer Towns, *Capturing A Town for Christ* (Old Tappan, NJ: Fleming H. Revell, Co., 1973), 48.

15. Ibid., 209.

16. Ibid., 212.

17. Ibid., 215.

18. Ibid., 80.

3. MICROPHONE MISSIONARY

1. Ben Bagdikian, *Media Monopoly* (Boston, MA: Beacon Press, 2000), 39.

2. Falwell and Towns, *Capturing a Town for Christ*, 59.

3. No byline, "Church Launches Alcoholic Home Project On Farm," *The News*, February 12, 1959: B1.

4. Falwell and Towns, *Capturing a Town for Christ*, 16–17.

5. Dinesh D'Souza, *Falwell: Before the Millennium* (Chicago: Regnery Gateway, 1984), 83.

6. Robert Ajemian, "Jerry Falwell Spreads the Word," *Time*, September 12, 1985.

7. Falwell and Towns, *Capturing a Town for Christ*, 80.

8. Falwell, *Falwell: An Autobiography*, 17.

9. Falwell and Towns, *Capturing a Town for Christ*, 60.

10. Ruth McClellan, *An Incredible Journey: Thomas Road Baptist Church and 50 Years of Miracles* (Lynchburg, VA: Liberty University, 2006), 239.

11. Jere Real, "Falwell U," *The Phoenix,* August 3, 2006, http://thephoenix.com/article_ektid19399.aspx.

12. Jeffrey K. Hadden and Charles E. Swann, *Prime Time Preachers* (Reading, MA: Addison-Wesley Publishing Co., 1981), 55.

13. McClellan, *An Incredible Journey,* 162.

14. Jerry Falwell, *Building Dynamic Faith* (Nashville, TN: World Publishing, 2005), 171.

15. McClellan, *An Incredible Journey,* 180.

16. Patrick MacDonald, "The Power and the Glory, the Rock Concert Turns 40," *Seattle Times,* March 22, 1992: A section.

17. D'Souza, *Falwell: Before the Millennium,* 100.

18. Ibid., 101.

4. BIBLICAL BLING

1. Susan Friend Harding, *The Book of Jerry Falwell* (Princeton, NJ: Princeton University Press, 2000), 107.

2. Direct-mail solicitation, August 13, 1981, for *The Old Time Gospel Hour,* by Jerry Falwell.

3. Patricia Pingry, *Jerry Falwell: A Man of Vision* (Milwaukee, WI: Ideals Publishing), 20.

4. Hadden and Swann, *Prime Time Preachers,* 51.

5. Ibid.

6. Cal Thomas and Ed Dobson, *Blinded By Might* (Grand Rapids, MI: Zondervan Publishing House, 1999), 22.

7. Ibid., 59.

8. Ibid.

9. Falwell and Towns, *Capturing a Town for Christ,* 72.

10. Falwell, *Falwell: An Autobiography,* 469.

5. MAGIC CITY

1. "Do It" speech before the National Religious Broadcasters Convention in Washington, D.C., February 2, 1987.

2. Rita Koselka, "Fear and Salvation," *Forbes,* June 1, 1987: 38.

3. Murray Waas, "The Falwell Connection," *Salon,* http://www.salon.com/news/1998/03/cov_11news.html.

7. IMMACULATE INFLECTION

1. Ron Brown, "Former Muslim to Head Seminary," *News & Advance,* February 15, 2005: A1.

2. Jim Langford and Jeremy Langford, *The Spirit of Notre Dame* (New York: Doubleday, 2005), 85.

3. Ibid., 14.

4. Ibid.

5. Ibid., 149.

6. Ibid., 168.

7. Alan L. Gillen, *The Genesis of Germs* (Green Forest, AR: Master Books, 2007).

8. Ibid.

9. Evelyn Martinique Mervine, comment on "Young Earth Creationists Are Not Geologists," *Memoirs of a Skepchick* blog, posted February 13, 2007, http://skepchick.org/blog/?p=396.

8. LORDS OF LYNCHBURG

1. Laurent, *A City Unto Itself,* 191.

2. Ibid, 194.

9. FALWELL 2.0

1. *Friends of God: A Road Trip with Alexandra Pelosi,* HBO Home Video (U.S. release date, October 9, 2007).

2. Transcript, "Myths of the Modern Mega-Church," The Pew Forum on Religion and Public Life, May 23, 2005.

3. David D. Kirkpatrick, "The Evangelical Crackup," *New York Times Magazine,* October 28, 2007: 38.

4. Ron Brown, "Bearing Gifts," *News & Advance,* September 4, 2005: A1.

5. Ron Brown, "Cash Donation Turns into Unique Task," *News & Advance,* September 4, 2005, B1.

Bibliography

Applegate, Debby. *The Most Famous Man in America: The Biography of Henry Ward Beecher*. New York: Three Leaves Press, 2006.

Beecher, Henry Ward. *The Life of Jesus the Christ*. New York: J. B. Ford and Co., 1871.

Bagdikian, Ben. *The Media Monopoly*, 6th ed. Boston: Beacon Press, 2000.

Barlow, Fred. *Profiles in Evangelism*. Murfreesboro, TN: Sword of the Lord, 1976.

Chambers, Osward. *My Utmost for His Highest*. Grand Rapids, MI: Discovery House Publishers, 1992.

Chambers, S. Allen. *Lynchburg: An Architectural History*. Charlottesville: University of Virginia Press, 1981.

Christian, W. Asbury. *Lynchburg and Its People*. Lynchburg, VA: J. P. Bell Co., 1900.

Dennis, Everette E. *Of Media and People*. Newbury Park, CA: Sage Publications, 1992.

Donovan, John B. *Pat Robertson: The Authorized Biography*. New York: Macmillan Publishing Co., 1988.

D'Souza, Dinesh. *Falwell: Before the Millennium*. Chicago: Regnery Gateway, 1984.

Elson, James M. *Lynchburg, Virginia: The First 200 Years, 1786 to 1986*. Lynchburg, VA: Warwick House Publishers, 2004.

Emery, Edwin and Michael Emery. *The Press and America: An Interpretive History of the Mass Media*, 5th ed. Englewood Cliffs, NJ: Prentice-Hall, Inc., 1984.

Falwell, Jerry. *Building Dynamic Faith*. Nashville, TN: World Publishing, 2005.

―――. *Falwell: An Autobiography*. Lynchburg, VA: Liberty House Publishers, 1997.

―――. *Listen America!* New York: Bantam Books, 1981.

――― and Elmer Towns. *Capturing a Town for Christ*. Old Tappan, NJ: Fleming H. Revell, 1973.

――― and Elmer Towns. *Church Aflame*. Nashville, TN: Impact Books, 1971.

Falwell, Jerry and Elmer Towns, eds. *Fasting Can Change Your Life*. Ventura, CA: Regal Books, 1998.

Gallup, George Jr., and Jim Castelli. *The People's Religion: American Faith in the 1990s*. New York: Macmillan, 1989.

Gilgoff, Dan. *The Jesus Machine: How James Dobson, Focus on the Family, and Evangelical America Are Winning the Culture War*. New York: St. Martin's Press, 2007.

Green, John C., Mark J. Rozell, and Clyde Wilcox, eds. *The Christian Right in American Politics: Marching to the Millennium*. Washington DC: Georgetown University Press, 2003.

Hadden, Jeffrey K. and Charles E. Swann. *Prime Time Preachers*. Reading, MA: Addison-Wesley Publishing Co., 1981.

Harding, Susan Friend. *The Book of Jerry Falwell: Fundamentalist Language and Politics*. Princeton, NJ: Princeton University Press, 2000.

Johnson, Robert Underwood and Clarence Clough Buel, eds. *The Way to Appomattox, Battles and Leaders of the Civil War*, vol. IV. New York: Thomas Yoseloff, 1956.

Kuo, David. *Tempting Faith: An Inside Story of Political Seduction*. New York: Free Press, 2006.

LaHaye, Tim and Jerry B. Jenkins. *Left Behind: A Novel of the Earth's Last Days*. Wheaton, IL: Tyndale House Publishers, 1995.

Langford, Jim and Jeremy Langford. *The Spirit of Notre Dame*. New York: Doubleday, 2005.

Laurant, Darrell. *A City Unto Itself*. Lynchburg, VA: The News and Advance, 1997.

Liebman, Robert C. and Robert Wuthnow, eds. *The New Christian Right*. Hawthorne, NY: Aldine Publishing Co., 1983.

Marsden, George M. *Reforming Fundamentalism: Fuller Seminary and the New Evangelicalism*. Grand Rapids, MI: William B. Eerdmans, 1987.

Martin, William. *With God On Our Side: The Rise of the Religious Right in America*. New York: Broadway Books, 1996.

McClellan, Ruth. *An Incredible Journey: Thomas Road Baptist Church and 50 Years of Miracles*. Lynchburg, VA: Liberty University, 2006.

Muller, George. *The Autobiography of George Muller*. New Kensington, PA: Whitaker House, 1985.

Noll, Mark. *The Scandal of the Evangelical Mind*. Grand Rapids, MI: William B. Eerdmans, 1994.

Pingry, Patricia. *Jerry Falwell: A Man of Vision.* Milwaukee, WI: Ideals Publishing, 1980.

Schaeffer, Francis A. *How Should We Then Live? The Rise and Decline of Western Thought and Culture.* Old Tappan, NJ: Fleming H. Revell, 1976.

Scofield, C. I. *The Scofield Reference Bible.* New York: Oxford University Press, 1909.

Smith, Rixey and Norman Beasley. *Carter Glass: A Biography.* New York: Longmans, Green and Co., 1939.

Spencer, Chauncey. *Who Is Chauncey Spencer?* Detroit, MI: Broadside Press, 1975.

Thomas, Cal and Ed Dobson. *Blinded By Might.* Grand Rapids, MI: Zondervan Publishing House, 1999.

Tucker, George. *The Life of Thomas Jefferson, Third President of the United States: With Parts of His Correspondence Never Before Published, and Notices of His Opinions On Questions of Civil Government, National Policy and Constitutional Law,* vol. I. Philadelphia, PA: Carey, Lea & Blanchard, 1837.

Viemeister, Peter. *The Beale Treasure: New History of a Mystery.* Bedford, VA: Hamilton's, 1997.

White, Mel. *Religion Gone Bad: The Hidden Dangers of the Christian Right.* New York: Jeremy P. Tarcher/Penguin, 2006.

Wills, Garry. *Mr. Jefferson's University.* Washington DC: National Geographic Society, 2002.

Woolley, Benjamin. *Savage Kingdom: The True Story of Jamestown, 1607, and the Settlement of America.* New York: HarperCollins Publishers, 2007.

Worsham, Kathleen Bonnie. *The Cedars of Cifax: A Virgina Rural Historic District.* Lynchburg, VA: Warwick House Publishing, 1997.

Index